Deep W
Secrecy and S

*

By Conrad J(
& Alan Pea

*

ISBN: 9781520682334

v 4:00

www.alanpearce.com

Disclaimer

This book is for educational purposes only. In no way is it the intention of the author, publishers or distributors to encourage anyone to do anything illegal. The author, publishers and distributors accept no liability for anything that happens in any way connected with the reading, possession or use of this book.
Don't even think about it.

Table of Contents

How to search the Surface and Deep Webs more effectively.

Why We Need Worry

Major threats come not from the National Security Agency or Britain's spy agency GCHQ but from cyber-criminals, business competitors, law firms, debt collectors, private investigators, stalkers and malicious trolls.

From the word go, we should all be alert to the dangers of the digital world. In the same way that children are made fearful of strangers and taught how to cross the road, we should all have cyber-safety drilled into us. The risks are everywhere and everybody is at risk.

Everybody under the age of 20 has grown up with the Internet but many fail to comprehend the dangers of opening their lives to all and sundry. Adults who give it any thought tend at best to install some anti-spyware and leave it at that. Few understand the depth of the risks or appreciate just how many people are really out to get them.

Cyber-Criminals

These days the streets are safer because so many criminals are migrating to digital and launching attacks from the comfort of their own homes.

If they haven't got the necessary skills, they can easily hire someone that has. There are hackers offering the complete service – from gaining access to a Google account, to stuffing a target's computer with images of child sexual abuse and then anonymously tipping off the police.

Increasingly, as better counter-spy tools come on the market, the bad guys are targeting the weakest link in the chain: the Human. They do this by so-called "Social Engineering", the art of making people do what they want them to do, from opening an infected attachment, to following a link on Twitter to a malicious website.

There are no limits to the forms this can take. Most professional con-artists now work online full time. They tug at the heart strings on dating sites, they offer amazing bargains, and they can pretend to be you in a crisis; imploring the friends in your contact book to send money urgently.

You might follow a link and take onboard a "Drive-By Download", a malicious program delivered in the same way as a regular cookie. The more sophisticated "Watering Hole Attacks" plant the malicious download in an advertising banner on a legitimate site. As soon as the page loads, the visiting device is infected.

The fastest growth-area for cyber-criminals is mobile. The smartphone is the finest tracking device ever devised. It can show where you are now and where you have been. It contains all your appointments, past and present, all your friends and private conversations. They can see what interests you, what you watch, buy and download, and they can turn on the camera and watch you.

Malicious programs enter the device via attachments, downloads, phony updates and even by simply viewing an image that automatically launches malware. Additionally, someone with access to the device can download and install a spy program that runs secretly in the background.

Even at the lowest level, the apps we download can be downright dangerous. Apps are dirt cheap or free because the developers make their money by letting in the advertising networks and criminals. It is true when they say "If you're not paying, you're the product".

Malicious apps have been found on iTunes and the Google App Store, and spyware has been found hidden within anti-spyware apps. There are apps that seek out financial transactions, others that suck up all the photos and look for points of blackmail.

A criminal may take possession of your devices and plant a "Botnet" which then runs unobtrusively to mine digital currencies like the BitCoin for somebody else's benefit. Others simply make calls to premium rate numbers and rack up your bill.

Business Competitors

All large corporations employ their own Intelligence agents. They want to know what their competitors are up to and to keep track of their employees, they want to know what is being said about them, and they want to know if anyone is selling secrets.

But it's not just the big boys; today any size business can employ the tools and techniques of a master-spy agency. Mobile communications can be intercepted, key-strokes logged, confidential reports copied, staff monitored and customers poached.

The business may employ a hot IT guy, but the criminal will always find a backdoor. A hacker employing 'social engineering' skills may surreptitiously drop a USB thumb drive marked Private in the hope that an inquisitive employee will slot it into an office machine to take a look. Result: instant infection. A CEO may be targeted via his outside interests and a way found into his phone or laptop.

Conversely, many companies inadvertently post confidential information online that can easily be retrieved by those that know how (see Deep Search).

Stalkers

It's no longer necessary to hide in the bushes when today's stalker can sip a *latte* at Café Nero and follow multiple victims in real time via the free Wi-Fi.

Download for free the suitably-named Creepy surveillance tool and you can keep close tabs on any active Twitter or Instagram user, following them on a map, seeing who they meet and much else. Conversely, acquire the victim's Google log-in and see their location history on Google Maps to follow their every move.

Or borrow someone's phone for a few minutes and secretly install a subscription-based surveillance package allowing the stalker to follow the GPS signal, listen in on conversations, read text and emails, examine images, videos and Skype calls, check Web habits, log passwords, block callers or outgoing numbers, and activate the microphone and camera. Packages start at just US$49 a month.

Another way in is to hoodwink the victim into inadvertently installing a *Remote Access Trojan* (RAT) which does much the same as the snooping package above. Sometimes people are tricked into opening *Remote Access* in *Settings* or by opening an infected attachment or by visiting a dodgy website. Anyone foolish enough to fall for this form of 'social engineering' can expect to have their devices taken over by some sick and disturbed people. Go to Youtube.com and type in *RAT + troll* and see how disturbing this can be.

The term "Internet of Things" (IOT) refers to all those other things connected to the Internet: refrigerators and domestic lighting, security cameras and door locks, for example. One simple way for an intruder to gain control of these devices is via the domestic router that channels the Wi-Fi and other digital connections.

The default Username for many of these devices is often "admin" and the Password "1234" or "password". Anybody within range with the right program on their laptop or tablet – such as the Angry IP Scanner which seeks out vulnerabilities – can gain total control of IOT devices and log all Internet activity. However, the passwords can easily be reset by following the manufacturer's instructions but few people ever bother.

Who Does this Concern?

The short answer is everybody who uses the Internet.

"It's a constantly increasing list and one that we're not even aware of today. I would say lawyers, doctors, investigators, possibly even accountants. Anyone who has an obligation to protect the privacy interests of their clients is facing a new and challenging world and we need new professional training and new professional standards to make sure that we have mechanisms to ensure that the average member of our society can have a reasonable measure of faith in the skills of all the members of these professions." – *Edward Snowden 17 July 2014 in The Guardian*.

All sophisticated security services monitor Internet traffic within their own countries. The US monitors *all* Internet traffic.

Legally, just the bare bones of the communications are monitored, the so-called Metadata – the who sent what and when. But, although they may not be open about this, many agencies are now looking directly into the message itself, looking for the expected and the unexpected in all our online communications and activities.

But don't suppose actual agents are used for such mundane tasks. Algorithms of stunning complexity analyze literally every word. And, when certain triggers are pulled, the surveillance moves up a notch and so on until it enters the physical world.

According to the US government's most recent figures, 4.8 million people now have security clearance that allows them to access all kinds of personal information, while 1.4 million people have *Top Secret* clearance – people like Edward Snowden and other private contractors.

The National Security Agency intercepts and stores the data from over 3 billion emails and other communications each day in its attempts to predict wrong-doing in what it terms the "paradigm of prevention" or "predictive policing"; and each day more than 1,600 people have their names added to the FBI's terrorism watchlist.

The US National Counterterrorism Center collects information on *every* US citizen and mines it for terrorism indicators. Agencies like the CIA collect all the data they can and then they store it indefinitely. If they ever need to join the dots, it helps to have all the dots from the past to draw upon.

If they have someone in their sights, the bad guys then insert malware into the smartphone or computer and take remote control; listening in on conversations, intercepting SMS and VoIP calls, and noting everything.

Nothing escapes their attention. There is a school of thought that the most successful companies got where they are today with a little outside help.

Imagine starting a service where millions of people will openly detail their lives and speak their minds. Then imagine being approached by an organization that would like to help you become a global brand. All you have to do in return is add a 'backdoor' allowing them direct access to the real names, physical addresses and activity logs of everybody who signs up.

If you don't play ball, well, your business will go nowhere and you might find that suddenly your credit cards don't work and then things begin to spiral downwards for you. It's not really an option. You build a backdoor. That's the theory.

When Briton Leigh Van Bryan, 26, planned a vacation to Hollywood, he tweeted friends that he planned to "destroy America", meaning in London-slang that he was going to have a jolly good time. The Department of Homeland Security didn't see it that way and were ready and waiting for him when he landed at Los Angeles Airport. He was handcuffed, interrogated for hours, locked in the cells overnight and unceremoniously deported.

They knew everything about him except what he was actually talking about. Algorithms may be smart but they just don't get the nuances. It's the little things like this which can set a suspicious mind off on a very deep investigation or drag you quickly off to a window-less cell. And this is why everybody should worry.

It's the same with email. If you don't believe that every word you write is scrutinized, try typing into an email the words, *bomb kill Trump Tuesday* and see how long it takes for them to come and get you.

The emails you receive can be equally dangerous. Anything that contains an image or link in HTML format, not to mention attachments, could result in a tracking device, key-logger or a beacon being inserted into your device, alerting the sender to your presence and precisely where you are sitting at that very moment.

Trackers are everywhere. Pay a visit to Twitter or Facebook and they will instantly plant little robots that follow you around, noting everything you do. To scoop up everybody else, the agencies channel users through a series of 'black boxes' or inspection points scattered around the net which then read everything that passes through them, analyzing it, logging it, storing it for deeper examination, or marking it for further attention.

With this so-called Deep Packet Inspection (DPI), all Internet traffic can be read, copied or modified, as can websites. DPI can also see who is uploading or downloading, what is inside and who is looking for it. Websites can be blocked and so can specific items within sites such as a particular video on YouTube.

Under the PRISM program, the NSA is apparently able to access the servers of at least nine leading US providers, including Google, Facebook and Microsoft. The companies themselves would not necessarily know that they had been compromised.

But this is small-fry. The US – along with its Five Eyes cyber-partners Britain, Canada, Australia and New Zealand – taps directly into undersea and fiber optic cables as well as communications satellites, taking the data from the source. The result is that virtually everything which travels on the Surface Internet, and much else, is open to inspection.

Now the Community Comprehensive National Cybersecurity Initiative Data Center in Utah, code-named Bumblehive, is on-stream, capturing all communication globally, including the complete contents of private emails, cell phone calls and Internet searches, plus all the personal data trails from parking receipts, bank transfers, travel itineraries and bookstore purchases. Another NSA data facility is already under construction in Maryland.

Data storage is remarkably cheap and getting cheaper every year. Analyzing and storing it all is now a cost-effective reality. The CIA proudly admits that "it is nearly within our grasp to compute on all human generated information."

Today everything is connected, everything communicates and everything is a sensor. Technology is moving so fast that even the major agencies can't keep up. Put all these things together and the inanimate becomes sentient and capable of decision-making. Suddenly the great dystopian fear is a reality.

And this is how they profile us all. It's been happening for years in the commercial world. Only when you appear to step out of line, say the wrong thing or spend too long looking at a bad kind of wiki, will you become interesting to the suspicious minds.

But mistakes are easily made in a world overseen by computers and not so easily rectified, as Mikey Hicks of New Jersey knows well. Every time he tries to fly, he is detained and thoroughly searched. Mikey is 13 years old and has been on the No-Fly List since he was two.

As it turns out, the bad guys don't say *kill* or *bomb* in their emails or on Twitter. The terrorists and super-criminals are not so dumb. They can also hire the smartest brains in the IT world and they pay better.

According to the US National Academy of Sciences, whilst data mining may work in the commercial world, it simply isn't feasible to prevent atrocities because terrorists don't use a one size fits all model; they change and adapt their *modus operandi* as they go along, preventing the algorithms from picking out a pattern.

Curiously, governments and intelligence agencies know this, too.

1. Taking Control

Everything you do on the Internet – every site you visit, every image or file you download, every email or message you send or receive – is logged on a computer somewhere. In a perfect world, we wouldn't need to worry. But this is not a perfect world.

Out there, someone or something is going through your personal data right now. Sometimes it's fairly harmless, like wanting know your shopping habits or eating preferences. Other times it's a lot more sinister.

From totalitarian regimes to outwardly democratic governments, there is a clamor for access to people's personal data. They want to read your emails and they want to know who your friends are. They want control, and the fear of terror, super criminals and child molesters provides sufficient justification.

The commercial world also poses a major threat. Personal information is a commodity today. It's bought and sold and analyzed, and then it's used to profile you for advertisers, campaign organizers, governments and criminals, stalkers and trolls.

While some people believe the Internet has set them free, many fear we are all voluntarily plugged into the finest surveillance apparatus ever devised.

"The internet, our greatest tool of emancipation, has been transformed into the most dangerous facilitator of totalitarianism," insists WikiLeaks founder Julian Assange.

"Within a few years, global civilization will be a postmodern surveillance dystopia, from which escape for all but the most skilled individuals will be impossible," he warns.

But none of this need happen. This book will show you how to protect yourself for the Internet of today and of tomorrow. The Internet was never conceived to be the preserve of commercial interests. It should not be a hunting ground for law enforcement. The time has come to take back control.

Entering Pioneer Territory

Some people will be surprised to learn that there is in fact another Internet, a Parallel Web much like the one we know with all the usual features like email, websites, bulletin boards, forums and social networks.

The difference is that the users of this Parallel Internet are doing everything anonymously. No one knows who they are or where they live. They cannot be tracked or profiled or analyzed.

This is the Deep Web – pioneer territory with very few settlers; perhaps 500,000 daily users at best compared to the 3 billion plus who stay up top. Some of the natives are hostile because they would rather keep the place to themselves. Others are friendly because they know more users mean more people to hide among.

Some say this Deep Web is more than 5,000 times the size of the Surface Web – so deep that the major search engines don't venture down there.

And then within this Deep Web are the Hidden Networks.

And it's by using these Hidden Networks – like the Tor Onion Router – that people can hide themselves. They do this by wearing a mask and by scrambling every bit of data they access, send or receive.

They can visit banned websites and they can travel the Surface Web anonymously. If they want, they can stay below to talk freely or express views that might otherwise offend. Many look to change the world.

Curiously, one might wonder why governments and the like are going to all the trouble of tracking us and storing our data, especially when they are ostensibly trying to catch pedophiles and terrorists.

As it happens, these people – the really bad guys – are not using the Surface Web to communicate. They are already *very* Deep and well ahead of the game. A cynic might wonder if there were ulterior motives in wanting to keep such tight tabs on us all.

But tell someone that you know how to go off-radar on the Internet and, as a rule, they won't believe you. They imagine the Feds or whoever have state-of-the-art technology and can see everything you do.

No doubt they do have amazing technology, but the remarkable thing here is just how simple it is to mix and match the different technologies available to make it seriously impossible for an adversary to find you.

Simply put, if they don't know where to look they really are not going to find you.

But you don't need to be a terrorist or up to no good to want to keep your online activities to yourself. Lots of people don't like being followed or having their mail read. Why can't ordinary people be anonymous, too?

Rather like books, who is to say a website should be banned, and who is to say that you cannot look at it?

We are now going to use the secrets of the Deep Web to help protect you and your family, your private and business interests, your views and your freedoms.

Going Down

So, how do we get there?

You need to know the entry points and you need to make a few adjustments to your computer, nothing difficult or damaging. All of this will be explained in the simplest way possible as we go on. The Deep Web is open to all of us, not just those who know how to write algorithms or speak programing languages.

In the following pages you will learn how to access the Deep Web and make yourself if not invisible, then certainly nigh impossible to find. You will learn how to blog and post anonymously and how to erase and hide your activities, set up a range of secure communications that nobody can intercept, avoid the attention of Big Business and other adversaries; hide and encrypt anything, and transfer and store information without anyone even knowing you are doing it. And lots of other useful things, too.

A technical aside

We are living in a constantly-changing game of cat and mouse. Techniques that might work today might not work tomorrow. In the brief period since this book was first published, a number of groups offering cyber-security and counter-surveillance technology have been forced out of business. Still more come online each week. We endeavor to keep this book as up-to-date as possible. If, however, you find that any of the techniques offered here are no longer valid, please let us know as soon as possible so we can launch an update.

Depending on the format of this book, all of the links given here should open in your browser. Deep Web links marked <!> can only be opened in a Tor-Firefox browser, which you will learn to configure shortly.

This book generally concerns itself with the Windows operating system because this is the most popular world-wide. However, where applicable, instructions for Mac and Linux systems are also given.

Macs and more recent Windows machines may have trouble installing some of the free software out there because they want you to use their products. Where possible, other options or work-arounds are given.

Be alert that no single system or piece of software is 100% secure or safe. However, by combining the techniques in the following pages, it is possible to operate in such a way that nobody ever need know what you are up to.

It is safe to assume that if law enforcement or the intelligence agencies want to monitor anybody's Internet access – read their emails and social media postings, find out what they are searching for and downloading, and listen in to their calls – then they can, regardless of the niceties of court orders and warrants. This means that absolutely everything is open to inspection.

In the final scene of the movie "Raiders of the Lost Ark", they place the Ark of the Covenant inside a crate and then they hide it inside a vast warehouse full of identical crates. This is the principle by which to operate, but on an infinitely vaster scale – down in the Deep Web.

Don't think of a needle in a haystack. Think of a needle in a universe of haystacks.

2. The Family

Let's imagine a simple scenario. You have a family and you all use the Internet. But you don't want anyone making use of the data trail you leave behind.

On one level, there are embarrassing things you would rather no one knew about. Just because you once looked up hemorrhoids on Google, you don't want to be bombarded with Preparation H advertisements every time you open a browser.

But you have deeper worries.

You do not like the idea of Microsoft and Yahoo! selling off your personal data to political campaign groups and others. And you don't even want to think what Google may know about you – or how easily they hand over your data to law enforcement.

You feel uncomfortable that private companies scour the Web for every scrap of information they can find about you, adding it to giant data-bases that link your voting history to your income, education and shopping preferences, and then selling off your digital life so you can be micro-targeted with tailor-made ads.

Perhaps you are not happy that your government has passed laws that allow its agents to comb through your emails, texts and other online correspondence and private files looking for signs of criminal activity or profiling you the way they do in the movie Minority Report.

And then you fear all the cyber criminals who are trying to hunt down your user log-ins and passwords to access your bank accounts and steal your money.

Cybercriminals make the most of news events and consumer trends to draw people to a webpage where malware will automatically plant itself in the computer, known as a "drive-by download". Malware can also be surreptitiously planted in legitimate websites to infect even the wary. These are known as "watering hole" attacks.

Within hours of any terrorist atrocity, the spammers send out emails and Twitter links seemingly from CNN and other sources which send users to sites compromised by Blackhole Exploit Kits and infection by Trojans, backdoors, infostealers or rootkits.

The same thing happens around most major news stories. And it's not just the gullible public who fall prey. Seasoned journalists are regularly sucked in with the apparent deaths of celebrities or by looming sex scandals.

Another growing threat is Ransomware, which locks a computer until a "fine" is paid. Infections often come via legitimate but compromised websites and advertisements where hackers have managed to insert malicious coding.

Victims suddenly find their screen frozen and a fake warning from the FBI or local law enforcement saying they have been downloading illegal content. Even more unnerving, the perpetrators occasionally include a mug shot from the victim's own webcam.

This malware is extremely hard to remove and, needless to say, once a fine has been paid the machine stays locked. Amusingly, a Chicago police department recently paid US$600 to hackers in a Ransomware sting.

If you have been the victim of the popular CoinVault Ransomware, help is at hand with the Kaspersky Ransomware Decryptor. Also try the Ransomware Response Kit.

Tracking people in cyberspace is child's play, especially when more than half of all Internet users have a page on Facebook. Big Data – Social, Mobile and Cloud – has altered the flow of information, overtaking traditional media.

Try typing your name into pipl.com and see just how much information comes up, and this is a free service with limited details. The paid-for services offer much more. And if you want to see just who is tracking you right now, install Lightbeam as an add-on to the Firefox browser.

With commercially-available software like Raytheon's social media data mining tool RIOT, simply enter a person's name and up pops a colorful graph showing where they have been, who they met and what they all look like. It then predicts their future movements

So what can you do?

Actually, it takes just a few minutes to tighten your security.

Browser — you will probably need to change your Web browser and make a few adjustments to the settings to stop websites stuffing your computer with cookies and tracking your every move, or remembering your passwords and browser history.

Email — if you don't want your email details sold off to all and sundry, you will find much safer options as we go on. You can also learn how to encrypt emails.

Anti-Virus — you *must* install software that keeps viruses and other nasties out of your computer.

Lock and Shred — personal documents should be stored in a locked folder. Laptops and other mobile devices should also be locked. Documents may need to be shredded, particularly when you dispose of an old device.

All these things are really easy and need not cost anything.

You can then take your security to Red Alert if you want. But, for now, let's just move you to Blue Alert.

Browser — start by dumping the Microsoft Explorer Web browser and install something less intrusive and more security conscious, such as Mozilla Firefox for Windows. There are also versions for Mac and Linux. Additionally, try Comodo's IceDragon for those who like Mozilla's Firefox and Comodo Dragon for those more familiar with the Google Chrome browser.

Once downloaded and installed, open the browser and change the security settings.

Click the browser's logo or *Settings* tab and select *Options/Options.*

In the dialog box, open *Privacy* then tick the option *Tell websites I do not want to be tracked.* There is an option to *Always use Private Browsing mode.* Untick *Accept cookies from sites.* Tick *Clear history when Firefox closes.* Under *History* select *Use custom settings for history* and select *Never remember history.*

Under *Security*, tick *Warn me when sites try to install add-ons.* Remove all exceptions. Tick *Block reported attack sites.* Tick *Block reported web forgeries.* Untick *Remember passwords for sites.*

On the *Advanced* tab, under *General* tick *Warn me when websites try to redirect or reload the page*. Under *Network* tick *Tell me when a website asks to store data for offline use*. Tick *Override automatic cache management* or set Cache Size to 0.

You can tighten things further with Blur for Firefox/IceDragon. This free app blocks Web beacons and trackers that advertisers and others use to observe your browsing habits. Once installed, a tiny icon in the top right corner issues an alert whenever a site has a bead on you.

A visit to Twitter will show that they allow over 5,000 different companies to follow your movements. At Facebook, nearly 8,000 will lock on and follow you around.

HTTPS Finder for Firefox/IceDragon automatically detects and enforces HTTPS connections when available, providing a reasonable guarantee that you are communicating with the intended website and not an imposter, plus ensuring that communications between the user and site cannot be read or forged by a third party. The Electronic Frontier Foundation has its own free version HTTPS Everywhere for Firefox, Dragon and Chrome browsers.

Next install Adblock Plus for Firefox/IceDragon. This free app allows you to block on-line ads from anyone you would rather not hear from. You can choose from a predefined list and you can personalize your own, but don't block sites you use regularly. Amazon, for example, is so stuffed with ads that by switching them off, the site instantly turns to text-only. You can also customize the settings to remove the annoying ads at the beginning of streaming videos on YouTube and elsewhere.

Also add on the BetterPrivacy app which allows you to remove or manage Flash-cookies set by Google, YouTube, eBay and others. Privacy+ does much the same thing. Flash plugins run independently of your browser and bypass any proxy configurations. If you were trying to mask your identity, these little nasties will reveal your IP address. Another good add-on is RequestPolicy which stops websites redirecting you unawares.

Firefox and other browsers have a *Private* browsing facility in the *Menu*. In this mode, the browser will not store any details of your travels and will help block tracking.

Perhaps the simplest solution for quick, secure browsing is to combine the *Private* mode with a 'gateway' service such as AllNetTools, Guardster or Anonymouse. These free services allow you to type in any Web address and then travel around without leaving a trace of your activities. These are particularly useful for sensitive search engines queries and for visiting locally banned websites.

Search Engines — obviously, Google keeps detailed records of your search queries, so select an engine which won't store your records. Options include the Secret Search Labs engine, DuckDuckGo
and iXQuick.

Email — with your browsing now sorted, you should think about dumping your email account if it's with Google, Yahoo! or any of the other big players and select one of the many free email providers who are less likely to sell off your personal details. You can connect these accounts, or multiples of accounts, to the email program that came bundled with your computer, and/or access the account directly on the Web. This last option being more secure.

You might also consider having more than one email account. You can use a separate account for linking to forums and social networks and then keep the private part of your life private.

Most infections come via email so it is important to put a few simple security measures in place. You should also disable the HTML settings in your email because when you open HTML emails they can transmit directly back to the sender, alerting them to your presence or confirming that you actually exist on the list of email addresses they purchased.

Generally, you can do this via the *Settings* tab. Look for and untick *Display attachments online* or tick *View message body as plain text*.

Virus — additionally, email can bring in all sorts of malware. Some of which can tap into your computer's microphone or webcam and send back a live transmission. Other malware will search inside your computer for passwords and sensitive data.

To keep these out, you should use a combination of standalone security software programs. See Avoiding Viruses, Trojans and Spyware to set up a seriously secure system.

System Security — Windows is an inherently insecure operating system which runs lots of unnecessary programs that can put your computer at risk, not to mention slowing it down. If you want to avoid people taking remote control of your computer or planting malware inside, you will need to tweak with some of the settings. This is not difficult and will take just three minutes. Here are guides for Windows, Mac and Linux.

Software — Microsoft's own software leaks like a sieve and is best replaced with the open source variety. MS Office records recently opened documents and even words in the documents. Windows Media Player logs every film you watch. PDF readers store a history of the files you read. They also collaborate with each other.

Use Open Office Suite instead of MS Office (Word, Excel, etc).

Use VLC Media Player instead of Windows Media Player.

Use Foxit PDF Reader instead of Adobe Acrobat Reader.

Shred — when it comes to removing files from your computer, you should install an eraser or shredder software. The Heidi Eraser is freeware that erases all files and traces of files. To erase all your tracks in one go, there is dedicated cleaning software like CCleaner, which is also free. Darik's Boot and Nuke (or DBAN) is an open-source program that permanently erases hard disks and entire systems. See Disc Encryption/Erasure.

Keep it simple — alternatively to downloading lots of different programs, you can bite the bullet and buy some excellent paid-for software. AVG Internet Security costs around $55 a year (it's cheaper than insurance) and includes firewall, anti-virus protection, anti-spam and anti-phishing, and dangerous website alerts. The free version is very good, too.

Smartphone — mobile is the fastest growing area of cyber-crime and you need pay special attention to avoid viruses and spyware. For Android users, the best free option is AVG Mobilation. With this, you can also track your phone on Google Maps (offering other possibilities) if it's stolen and lock it remotely.

For iPhone, iPad and iPod Touch, you can download the Anti-Virus & Malware Scanner which costs around $2.39. With this, you scan e-mail attachments and other files on your Apple device, or files on remote locations such as Dropbox and Web servers.

Downloading — this is, of course, the other most likely way to get an infection. Firewalls and anti-virus programs will generally keep you safe. If you are using the Firefox or IceDragon browsers, the free app DownThemAll helps manage your downloads, allowing you to switch on and off and resume the download, and is even said to speed things up 400%.

Some countries have introduced stringent anti-downloading laws that benefit businesses which haven't moved with the times, like the music and film industries. Sadly, innocent people can get caught up in this mess when downloading episodes they missed on TV or whatever. Torrent programs can easily trigger the attention of the monitoring authorities but there are safer alternatives (see Usenet Newsgroups).

Photos — if family members like to upload photos of themselves to the Web, you should know that most modern cameras and smartphones add GPS data to the image's EXIF file, allowing others to pin-point your location or haunts. You can check how much data is stored in a digital photo by uploading one to exifdata.com. To clean up images before you upload then, there are numerous free tools, including ExifTool and JHead.

Do all these things and you are now at Blue Alert, which will keep you safe from all but the most determined assaults. But, should you need to tighten things up still further, please read on.

---

3. The Blogger

Blogging is not generally illegal but people can lose their jobs through blogging and it can get you into trouble with the authorities and employers. So let's assume you want to blog and want to be as anonymous as possible.

By its very nature, a blog will give away certain elements of your personality but not necessarily your identity if you cover your tracks. That said, you can never guarantee your anonymity 100 percent because a determined adversary with unlimited resources will get you in the end. You can, however, make their lives extremely difficult.

Firstly, you should write under a pseudonym so pick something that doesn't connect to you. To start the ball rolling, you will need an anonymous email account which you can use to set up the anonymous blogging account. However, this email and the blog site will most likely log your IP address whenever you access the accounts and this will link to your physical address.

There are several ways around this. First, select email and blog hosts whose websites do not require JavaScript to be running on your browser because JavaScript will link back to you. Next, you might want to route all your traffic through a proxy service that obscures your IP address.

You can find a list of proxy servers on-line or visit Proxy4Free or the Rosinstrument Proxy Database. Select one marked *high anonymity* and make a note of the IP address and port setting. You will now need to make a few adjustments to your Web browser.

On Firefox/IceDragon, click *Tools, Internet Options, Connections, Settings*. Turn on *Manual Proxy Configuration*, enter the IP address of your chosen proxy server and the port number into the fields for HTTP proxy and SSL proxy, and then save. Now close and reopen the browser.

Keep a separate browser for regular on-line activities and the proxy one just for your blog. If you have more than one blog, use different email and blog hosts and think twice before embedding any social network links like Facebook or Twitter, or an RSS feed. Equally, never visit your blog from any device linked to you and never Tweet about it under your real identity.

In countries with Internet censorship, governments often block proxies which means you may have to keep changing proxies to stay one step ahead. Even then, governments with tight control over their country's Internet Service Providers (ISPs) can sift through their logs and discover which users are employing proxies and catch them that way.

The best way around this is to go Deep Web and use the Tor Hidden Network. This takes the proxy to a new level by not only hiding you among all the other users but repeatedly encrypting and unencrypting whatever data you send and receive. You will need to download the Tor/Firefox browser and fiddle with the settings. This is explained in full detail later in the book. See Using Hidden Networks.

Once on a Hidden Network, you can access the email and blog sites without leaving any trace of your IP address.

Better yet, go all James Bond and get a USB thumb drive and download the Tor/Firefox browser to the drive. You then plug this into any computer anywhere and access the Deep Web or go anonymously above. You might also add a number of simple apps to the drive, including text and photo editors and a shredder. Then shred relevant documents once the blog has been uploaded. Options include Eraser and Evidence Nuker. Also see Portable Access.

Be equally cautious in publicizing your blog. To get your message out use Pingomatic which will alert dozens of blog search engines including Google Blog Search and Technorati. You can select which engines you want to list your blog and specify specialized services such as audio blogs. It takes just a matter of minutes for your latest entry to be logged, cached and listed.

Conversely, you might not want anyone to know about your blog, bar a select few, and will want to keep it out of the search engines. Type "Robots Text File Generator" into Google or iXQuick or visit a site like Mcanerin International. Here you can enter your blog address and then select which if any engines you want to index your site. A *robots.txt* file is then created. You need to upload this file to your root directory to tell the engines whether they can come in or not. See the FAQ at your chosen blog host to see how to do this as techniques vary.

Equally, you might want to limit the people who can read your blog. Some blogging services allow you to do this; others have password protection, too.

But none of this is 100% bullet proof. A better option for safer blogging is to register your own domain name, but do so via an anonymous name registrar and then have it hosted elsewhere on an anonymous host. Search for services offering anonymous domains and hosting.

Putting together a simple website is easy. There are hundreds of programs that you can download, both free and paid for. If you are serious, consider Netobjects Fusion which is intuitive and easy to use.

If your own government is tenacious in these matters, you might register the domain and hosting contract in countries that don't have friendly relations with them. This will make any court order for disclosure meaningless.

Generally, if you want to know who owns a domain, you can look it up at WHOIS. Most registrars will give you the option of masking your WHOIS entry but, better still, anonymous name registrars will register the site in their name.

You then access all this from a public computer via Tor with an encrypted USB drive and nobody need be any the wiser.

However, investigators always follow the money, so paying by credit card or PayPal may lead them to you. As it happens, the Deep Web has its own currency, the apparently untraceable BitCoin, and there are hosting companies who accept them. Type bitcoin + hosting + domain into a search engine.

Another option is a pre-paid credit card. But, when all is said and done, there is no true hiding place. It's no secret that the security services can employ sophisticated algorithms to analyze any blog's writing style and idiosyncrasies. All they have to do then is compare the patterns with all the emails they intercept and simply pluck the culprit from among billions.

4. The Whistle Blower

Let's imagine now that you are a whistle blower. You have access to some terrible secret and you want the world to know about it but you don't want to get caught. You now need some serious security.

Let's also assume you have the data in digital format. You have two main options:

Post it on-line straight away, preferably to a secret discussion board on the Deep Web where lots of like-minded people will see it, and immediately destroy all evidence your end.

Or, make contact with a journalist or professional whistle-blowing organization and hand the incriminating evidence over.

The first option involves you entering a Hidden Network on the Deep Web so you will need to download the free Tor/Firefox bundle. This is a typical Mozilla Firefox browser but one configured to access the Tor Network and travel the Surface Web anonymously. To set this up, which takes less than five minutes and no special skills, see First Steps.

Once in the Deep Web, by cutting and pasting, you can upload vast quantities of text to any of several anonymous file hosting sites and leave no link back to yourself.

With the terrible secret now safely out of your hands, you should destroy the evidence your end with a file shredder or eraser program. Options include Eraser and Evidence Nuker.

Lastly, use an anonymous Deep Web message board to give out the link to the uploaded data and draw people's attention. Then let somebody else deal with it.

To be really safe, fully read the instructions further on for using Tor, together with encryption options. You may find this the safest way to blow your whistle.

The second option involves you making contact with somebody else and this is where it gets risky because you can't always trust people on the other end. Also, many of the whistle-blowing organizations – such as the National Whistle Blowers Centre in the US – ask for full contact details which, given anonymity is probably an issue, can put some people off.

The best option is to contact a likely journalist direct. But how do you make first contact without giving yourself away? Further down this book are many tools which will help you do just that but, for the moment, here is a simple solution.

Once you identify your journalist and you have their email address, go to a free email re-mailing service such as AnonyMouse and compose a message. Re-mailers strip off any codes that might identify you and add new ones along the journey. When the email arrives at its destination, there is no way that it can traced back to you.

With this email, whet their appetite about the terrible secret and enclose a link which takes them to PrivNote – a free app that allows you to compose a message that will promptly self-destruct once read. PrivNote generates a link which you pass on. You can also ask PrivNote for a read receipt.

The shear thought of a self-destructing message will get the attention of most journalists. Use this to tell them to join a Deep Web personal messaging system that you can find on the HiddenWiki. Also in the PrivNote message, give the journalist a return email address set up at a free service and ask them to reply, enclosing their new contact details.

When you receive their email, look at the delivery codes to confirm that the right person has answered your message.

You can now message them directly with a fair degree of confidence that your communications have not been intercepted and have reached the desired person. Once contact is fully established, be sure to both then encrypt your messages.

When transferring sensitive documents, do not give them names that identify the contents or attract unwanted interest; give them names like *GrandmasGoatHeadYohurtSoupRecipe.doc* or *MyDissertation.PDF*.

Increasingly, many news organizations are employing a system known as SecureDrop, from the Freedom of the Press Foundation that allows whistle blowers to send material anonymously. It also incorporates an encrypted messaging service.

For additional security, encrypt all messages and documents. See Encryption and Cryptography.

5. The Campaigner

Now let's suppose you are a campaigner. This could cover a variety of activities but let's say you live in a nice, quiet rural village where Big Business is about to drive a giant toll road right through the middle of town. You've been thwarted at every turn and now you want to protest.

You might find that whenever you plan a protest or demonstration, the police and private security guards are already there ahead of you. You will need to ensure that your on-line correspondence is secure.

An amusing way of sending secret messages is to hide them inside something so fundamentally boring that no one will bother to look deeper. Check out SpamMimic.

Here, you can enter a short message and have it re-generated as mind-numbing *spamtext* that you can send out via a free email service. Cut and paste the text below (including the last full stop) and feed it back into the decoder to get the hidden message:

Dear Friend ; Your email address has been submitted
to us indicating your interest in our publication .
If you no longer wish to receive our publications simply
reply with a Subject: of "REMOVE" and you will immediately
be removed from our club . This mail is being sent
in compliance with Senate bill 1916 ; Title 7 ; Section
302 . Do NOT confuse us with Internet scam artists
. Why work for somebody else when you can become rich
in 17 months ! Have you ever noticed people love convenience
& nobody is getting any younger ! Well, now is your
chance to capitalize on this . WE will help YOU sell
more and deliver goods right to the customer's doorstep
! You are guaranteed to succeed because we take all
the risk . But don't believe us . Mr Jones who resides
in South Dakota tried us and says "Now I'm rich many

---

more things are possible" . We assure you that we operate
within all applicable laws . We IMPLORE you - act now
. Sign up a friend and your friend will be rich too
! Warmest regards . Dear Friend , We know you are interested
in receiving amazing intelligence ! We will comply
with all removal requests . This mail is being sent
in compliance with Senate bill 2616 , Title 4 , Section
306 ! This is different than anything else you've seen
! Why work for somebody else when you can become rich
within 90 DAYS . Have you ever noticed more people
than ever are surfing the web & people love convenience
! Well, now is your chance to capitalize on this !
WE will help YOU increase customer response by 150%
plus process your orders within seconds . You can begin
at absolutely no cost to you ! But don't believe us
! Mrs Simpson of Iowa tried us and says "My only problem
now is where to park all my cars" ! We are licensed
to operate in all states ! We implore you - act now
. Sign up a friend and you'll get a discount of 70%
. Thank-you for your serious consideration of our offer
.

This is only good for short messages. PrivNote is good for
reams of text. Next you should consider encryption. A PGP
Key is the best way to do that. There are various ways of
setting up a PGP Key, see Encryption and Cryptography. You
can have it added on to an email program like Outlook, you
can run a stand-alone program.

You will need to generate two keys – a public key which you
give to anyone wanting to send you encrypted data and a
private key that you keep to yourself. The sender uses your
public key to encrypt the data and then sends it to you. When
you receive the data, you unscramble it with your private key.

Additionally, the Icelandic free email service unseen.is has a
facility allowing you to send and receive PGP encryption
emails with the minimum of complication. However, the
stand-alone systems tend to be more secure.

This will keep you moderately safe. There is no known way that an adversary can decrypt your messages without your private PGP key, so you might want to keep that very safe. However, a smart investigator could soon discover that you are sending encrypted emails and you might prefer that they didn't know.

In the United Kingdom and Australia, for example, recent laws oblige people under investigation to hand over their passwords or face a prison term comparable to that of carrying an illegal firearm.

You can store your own passwords in a variety of ways. There are dedicated password safes like KeePass that allow you to manage all your passwords in one place so you don't have to keep remembering different ones or, worst of all, use the same password for everything.

If a password safe can itself draw attention, you can hide passwords very simply by putting them in files where nobody is ever likely to look. Open any program on your computer and insert a file deep inside with an innocuous name, such as *Packets29T.txt*.

Now you might want to look at other, less obvious, means of communication. Re-mailers are very good for sending messages one way (they also take a while to be delivered) but for two-way communication other options are called for.

A very simple alternative is to open a free email account and then give the address and log-in details to the other members of your group. Messages are then written but saved as *Drafts* and never sent. The draft messages are then accessed by those with the password. This way the emails are never actually transmitted. You can even use the account as a personal bulletin board with all members posting on different topics. Additionally, you can encrypt messages to individuals. Do change addresses regularly as over-active draft boxes can arouse interest.

For secure group discussions and for sending encrypted messages among your group, consider Signal from Open Whisper Systems, which is free and open-source.

But things are starting to hot up. Big Business has you under observation. You really don't want to be doing any of these things at home or the office anymore.

If you have an older screen – a CRT cathode ray tube – on your computer, the bad guys can read what's on the screen by tuning in to your *compromising emanations*, basically radio signals that can be received by somebody sitting in a car outside or in a nearby building. You can put a stop to this by installing a free software program known as a Zero Emission Pad which will defuse the signals. For more modern screens, the authorities can bombard an area or room with a Continuous Microwave Generator that effectively connects the target computer to an outside monitor. An option here is to place a towel over your head to cover the screen.

And don't even think about taking your laptop outside and connecting to a public Wi-Fi network because these are all too easily monitored. If you must, an option here is to employ Hotspot Shield which encrypts all smartphone and tablet traffic through a Virtual Private Network (VPN) to mask your identity and prevent tracking. It also allows you to view banned content and access Twitter and Facebook mobile if their services are ever blocked locally.

Better yet, go Deep Web.

Download the Tor/Firefox browser and set it up, as explained in Using Hidden Networks, but install it directly to a USB thumb drive. You can now visit your local library or cybercafé and slip the USB into the machine. This will open a dialogue box to the drive. Select *Start Tor Browser* and you will leave no trace of your Web journey on the machine and no one will be able to track you.

From here you can access your shared email account or you can go truly Deep Web and do all your communications down there. A good, free option is BitMessage Mail Gateway, a Swiss-based Tor email service <!> http://bitmailendavkbec.onion/.

As tension increases and the bulldozers begin to move in, you might want to hide your important documents and contact lists well away from your computer and out of reach of the bad guys.

The great thing about the Deep Web is that it is mind-bogglingly enormous; so big, in fact, that looking for a single file is a bit like looking for an invisible needle in a universe of needles and then some.

Start off by putting your sensitive data inside a RAR or 7z file and then encrypt it using a strong password. If you want to hide a video file, you should first split it down into smaller, manageable portions using HJSplit, a free program that both splits and re-joins large files.

Single files can be uploaded to a Deep Web file host, of which there are many. Here, again, you can set password access to the file. Multiple files are best uploaded to different servers and each given different names. You will need to keep a note of what's what and where so you can eventually re-assemble them.

But you can go even further than this. The art of hiding things inside other things goes back to the dawn of time. People have hidden messages as Morse code inside knitting yarn sent to prisoners of war and microdots disguised as full stops in books. Today, we have some very modern equivalents.

You can hide any text document inside a digital photo. You can hide a short video inside a music track. This art is called *steganography* and there are a number of programs that can perform this magic, some free like QuickCrypto.

A possibility here is to use a given photo on a website as a hidden 'drop box' where people can come and collect their individual messages. You might, for example, give somebody instructions that are hidden inside a photo of an Abyssinian cat snoozing in the shade on a website full of exotic cats. Only that person who knows which photo to look for will be able to find it, and then open it.

An investigator, even one that suspects messages are being hidden inside photos, will have the devil's own job working out which one because outwardly they appear identical.

But things are getting out of hand now. Extremists have moved into the village and all Hell has broken loose. In a bid to stem the mayhem, the authorities force every ISP in the land to deny access to the social networks, particularly Twitter and Facebook, because the extremists are using them to organize and deploy themselves.

But, actually, you don't care. You can still access Twitter and Facebook with your Tor browser, and you can communicate and organize with your own group unhindered and unobserved by the bad guys because now they don't have access.

And then, suddenly, this is Red Alert – the whole village is in flames and you don't have a house or cybercafé anymore, and your computer and laptop have melted. But they still can't stop you because you had the foresight to set up a covert browser in your smartphone with apps for Android and iOS.

You can access anything you like because, as soon as you connect to the Web, you give the impression of being in a far-away country. Anything blocked in your homeland is easily available to you. You can still access your emails, chat on the forums and PM your friends. You can anonymously surf the Web – both of them.

Sadly, your home is charcoal and your village is covered in Tarmac® but you do have a nice swift highway to take you far, far away.

6. Using Hidden Networks

Now it's time to sort out Deep Web entry. There are several Hidden Networks. They may be hundreds but who knows? We are going to use the biggest of them all – Tor.

What is Tor? It stands for The Onion Router, so-called because of the layered encryption process. Tor was originally funded by the US Navy at the start of the Millennium and is used by numerous agencies and others to transmit and receive sensitive information.

You should use Tor for all your secret online activities.

To access Tor, you will first need a specially-configured Web browser which you can download shortly. This Tor-browser combination diverts Internet traffic through a worldwide volunteer network of servers to conceal a user's location and activities, effectively hiding users among all the other users. It works by encrypting and re-encrypting data multiple times as it passes through successive Tor relays. This way the data cannot be unscrambled in transit.

Tor does have its flaws and should not be considered completely safe. Although your IP address is concealed, a digital fingerprint can linger allowing someone accessing your local network –a Wi-Fi provider or an ISP working with criminals or law enforcement – to glean some idea of your activities.

Therefore, it is essential to first employ a VPN before activating Tor. This way you immediately disappear down a rabbit hole hiding your activities from the ISP before slipping unobserved onto the Tor network. Search for recommended secure VPNs and select one that stores no data on you.

The waters can be mudded even further for any eavesdropper by requesting more than one site at a time or by downloading more than one item simultaneously, and by regularly resetting the *Use a new identity* facility on the Tor control panel.

Certain plug-ins will not work on the Tor Browser such as Flash, RealPlayer and QuickTime as they can be manipulated into revealing an IP address.

First Steps
Begin by downloading the free Tor/Firefox bundle. This is safe, easy to install, and includes everything you need to begin a surreptitious journey. Simply follow the on-screen instructions and a gateway to the Deep Web can be configured in minutes with no special skills.

Be absolutely certain that you are downloading from the torproject.org website. A Hidden Network used in Iran was recently infiltrated when a fake version of their modified browser was distributed which gave away the identity of users.

As soon as Tor opens the Firefox browser, click the logo in the top left-hand corner and block scripts globally. Also, add an HTTPS enforcer to your browser, such as HTTPS Finder or HTTPS Everywhere.

Once loaded, the browser will display a very basic-looking Web page (the Deep Web resembles the Surface Web circa 1996) and the
words:

-

Congratulations. Your browser is configured to use Tor.
Please refer to the Tor website for further information about using
Tor safely. You are now free to browse the Internet anonymously.

-

You are now anonymous and free to explore the Onion Network or branch off to the Surface Web.

If you are in a country where ISPs or governments are able to block the Tor network, open *Settings* on the Tor dialogue box, select *Network*, and then tick the box *My ISP blocks connections to the Tor network*.

You are now given the option to *Add a Bridge* or *Find Bridge Now*. If no bridges (non-public relays) are found, go to the Tor bridge relay page on the Surface Web and select them manually by cutting and pasting until you find one that works for you. Add as many bridges as possible as this increases your chances of connecting and improves security.

Using Tor
Rather like time travel, this level of the Internet appears much as it did in the very early days, including the lengthy wait while pages load. There are no frills or flashy graphics, just simple text and images.

On Tor, people communicate secretly and securely. Whistle blowers and dissidents, activists and journalists, aid-workers and academics, criminals and terrorists all carry on their day-to-day activities.

Top secret papers along the lines of WikiLeaks are posted here, as are guides and wikis for every type of activity, legal and otherwise; and all manner of unconventional views are expressed. Here you can lurk hidden and surreptitiously store any amount of data for free.

Tor has its own chat rooms, forums, blogs, file hosts, and many of the usual features of the Surface Web.

Deep Websites can disappear or fail to load from time to time. If you have difficulty opening a particular page, just try again later and it may reappear. Also, you may not be able to cut and paste from this e-book but, if you temporarily set Tor-Firefox as your default browser, all links will open directly into the Surface Web or Deep Web.

Entry Points

Recent activity by various government agencies, mostly in the USA and the UK, has seen a number of Hidden Services on Tor disappear. The links given below were active at the time of publication. We take no responsibility for the trustworthiness or reliability of the following Onion sites. Equally, they may not always be available.

The Hidden Wiki <!>
http://zqktlwi4fecvo6ri.onion/wiki/Main_Page often described as the hub of the Deep Web, this is the best starting point for new-comers. Here you can find lists of other hidden networks and links to black market goods and financial services, file hosts, blogs, forums, political groups and whistle-blowing boards. Beware that many of the traders here are pure scammers, so be very cautious before parting with any money. The wiki is available in 17 languages. Mirror sites: <!> http://wikitjerrta4qgz4.onion/ and <!> http://zqktlwi4fecvo6ri.onion/wiki/index.php/Main_Page. The Uncensored Hidden Wiki can be found at <!> http://gxamjbnu7uknahng.onion/wiki/index.php/Main_Page
TorLinks <!> torlinkbgs6aabns.onion links directory where you can add your own links and set up a Deep Website.
OnionDir <!> http://dirnxxdraygbifgc.onion/ Tor link directory.
OnionList <!> http://jh32yv5zgayyyts3.onion/ Onion link list and directory.
ParaZite Links List <!>
http://kpynyvym6xqi7wz2.onion/links.html

Onion URL Repository <!> http://32rfckwu0rlf4dlv.onion/
TorWiki <!>
http://torwikignoueupfm.onion/index.php?title=Main_Page

Deep Search Engines — Tor has a number but none are in any way comprehensive:
Ahmia Tor Search https://ahmia.fi
Torch <!> http://xmh57jrzrnw6insl.onion/
DuckDuckGo Search Engine <!>
http://3g2upl4pq6kufc4m.onion/

Marketplace Drugs <!>
https://www.deepdotweb.com/marketplace-directory/categories/top-markets/

Misc <!>
http://e266al32vpuorbyg.onion/bookmarks.php - Dark Nexus
http://5plvrsgydwy2sgce.onion/ - Seeks Search
http://2vlqpcqpjlhmd5r2.onion/ - Gateway to Freenet
http://nlmymchrmnlmbnii.onion/ - Is It Up?
http://kpynyvym6xqi7wz2.onion/links.html - ParaZite
http://wiki5kauuihowqi5.onion/ - Onion Wiki
http://torwikignoueupfm.onion/index.php?title=Main_Page
- Tor Wiki
http://kpvz7ki2v5agwt35.onion - The Hidden Wiki
http://idnxcnkne4qt76tg.onion/ - Tor Project: Anonymity
Online
http://torlinkbgs6aabns.onion/ - TorLinks
http://jh32yv5zgayyyts3.onion/ - Hidden Wiki .Onion Urls
http://wikitjerrta4qgz4.onion/ - Hidden Wiki - Tor Wiki
http://xdagknwjc7aaytzh.onion/ - Anonet Webproxy
http://3fyb44wdhnd2ghhl.onion/wiki/index.php?title=Main
_Page - All You're Wiki - clone of the clean hidden wiki that
went down with freedom hosting
http://3fyb44wdhnd2ghhl.onion/ - All You're Base
http://j6im4v42ur6dpic3.onion/ - TorProject Archive

http://p3igkncehackjtib.onion/ - TorProject Media
http://kbhpodhnfxl3clb4.onion - Tor Search
http://cipollatnumrrahd.onion/ - Cipolla 2.0 (Italian)
http://dppmfxaacucguzpc.onion/ - TorDir - One of the oldest
link lists on Tor

Marketplace Financial

http://torbrokerge7zxgq.onion/ - TorBroker - Trade securities
anonymously with bitcoin, currently supports nearly 1000
stocks and ETFs
http://fogcore5n3ov3tui.onion/ - Bitcoin Fog - Bitcoin Laundry
http://2vx63nyktk4kxbxb.onion/ - AUTOMATED PAYPAL
AND CREDIT CARD STORE
http://samsgdtwz6hvjyu4.onion - Safe, Anonymous, Fast,
Easy escrow service.
http://easycoinsayj7p5l.onion/ - EasyCoin - Bitcoin Wallet
with free Bitcoin Mixer
http://jzn5w5pac26sqef4.onion/ - WeBuyBitcoins - Sell your
Bitcoins for Cash (USD), ACH, WU/MG, LR, PayPal and
more
http://ow24et3tetp6tvmk.onion/ - OnionWallet - Anonymous
Bitcoin Wallet and Bitcoin Laundry
http://qc7ilonwpv77qibm.onion/ - Western Union Exploit
http://3dbr5t4pygahedms.onion/ - ccPal Store
http://y3fpieiezy2sin4a.onion/ - HQER - High Quality Euro
Replicas
http://qkj4drtgvpm7eecl.onion/ - Counterfeit USD
http://nr6juudpp4as4gjg.onion/pptobtc.html - PayPal to
BitCoins
http://nr6juudpp4as4gjg.onion/doublecoins.html - Double
Your BitCoins
http://lw4ipk5choakk5ze.onion/raw/4588/ - High Quality
Tutorials

Marketplace Commercial Services

http://6w6vcynl6dumn67c.onion/ - Tor Market Board -
Anonymous Marketplace Forums
http://wvk32thojln4gpp4.onion/ - Project Evil

http://5mvm7cg6bgklfjtp.onion/ - Discounted electronics goods

http://lw4ipk5choakk5ze.onion/raw/evbLewgkDSVkifzv8zAo/ - Unfriendlysolution - Legit hitman service

http://nr6juudpp4as4gjg.onion/torgirls.html - Tor Girls

http://tuu66yxvrnn3of7l.onion/ - UK Guns and Ammo

http://nr6juudpp4as4gjg.onion/torguns.htm - Used Tor Guns

http://ucx7bkbi2dtia36r.onion/ - Amazon Business

http://nr6juudpp4as4gjg.onion/tor.html - Tor Technology

http://hbetshipq5yhhrsd.onion/ - Hidden BetCoin

http://cstoreav7i44h2lr.onion/ - CStore Carded Store

http://tfwdi3izigxllure.onion/ - Apples 4 Bitcoin

http://e2qizoerj4d6ldif.onion/ - Carded Store

http://jvrnuue4bvbftiby.onion/ - Data-Bay

http://bgkitnugq5ef2cpi.onion/ - Hackintosh

http://vlp4uw5ui22ljlg7.onion/ - EuroArms

http://b4vqxw2j36wf2bqa.onion/ - Advantage Products

http://ybp4oezfhk24hxmb.onion/ - Hitman Network

http://mts7hqqqeogujc5e.onion/ - Marianic Technology Services

http://mobil7rab6nuf7vx.onion/ - Mobile Store

http://54flq67kqr5wvjqf.onion/ - MSR Shop

http://yth5q7zdmqlycbcz.onion/ - Old Man Fixer's Fixing Services

http://matrixtxri745dfw.onion/neo/uploads/MATRIXtxri745dfwONION_130827231336IPA_pc.png - PC Shop

http://storegsq3o5mfxiz.onion/ - Samsung StorE

http://sheep5u64fi457aw.onion/ - Sheep Marketplace

http://nr6juudpp4as4gjg.onion/betcoin.htm - Tor BetCoin

http://qizriixqwmeq4p5b.onion/ - Tor Web Developer

http://vfqnd6mieccqyiit.onion/ - UK Passports

http://en35tuzqmn4lofbk.onion/ - US Fake ID Store

http://xfnwyig7olypdq5r.onion/ - USA Citizenship

http://uybu3melulmoljnd.onion/ - iLike Help Guy

http://dbmv53j45pcv534x.onion/ - Network Consulting and Software Development

http://lw4ipk5choakk5ze.onion/raw/4585/ - Quick Solution (Hitman)
http://nr6juudpp4as4gjg.onion/tynermsr.htm - Tyner MSR Store

Hosting
http://matrixtxri745dfw.onion/ - Image Uploader
http://lw4ipk5choakk5ze.onion/ - PasteThis - Tor based Pastebin
http://wzrtr6gpencksu3d.onion:8080/ - Gittor
http://nr6juudpp4as4gjg.onion/ - Free hosting
http://tklxxs3rdzdjppnl.onion/ - Liberty's Hackers Hosting Service
http://matrixtxri745dfw.onion/ - Matrix Trilogy

Blogs
http://74ypjqjwf6oejmax.onion/ - Beneath VT - Exploring Virginia Tech's Steam Tunnels and Beyond
http://76qugh5bey5gum7l.onion/ - Deep Web Radio
http://edramalpl7oq5npk.onion/Main_Page - Encyclopedia Dramatica
http://ih4pgsz3aepacbwl.onion/ - Hushbox
http://ad52wtwp2goynr3a.onion/# - Dark Like My Soul
http://tns7i5gucaaussz4.onion/ - FreeFor
http://gdkez5whqhpthb4d.onion/ - Scientology Archive
http://newsiiwanaduqpre.onion/ - All the latest news for tor
http://5vppavyzjkfs45r4.onion/ - Michael Blizek
http://7ueo7ahq2xlpwx7q.onion/ - AYPSELA News
http://7hk64iz2vn2ewi7h.onion/ - Blog about Stories
http://tigas3l7uusztiqu.onion/ - Mike Tigas
http://mpf3i4k43xc2usxj.onion/ - Sam Whited
http://7w2rtz7rgfwj5zuv.onion/ - An Open Letter to Revolutionaries
http://3c3bdbvhb7j6yab2.onion/ - Totse 2
http://4fvfamdpoulu2nms.onion/ - Lucky Eddie's Home
http://nwycvryrozllb42g.onion/searchlores/index.htm - Fravia's Web Searching Lore

http://newsiiwanaduqpre.onion/ - OnionNews - Blog about the onionland

Forums and Chans

http://2gxxzwnj52jutais.onion/phpbb/index.php - Onion Forum 2.0 renewed

http://3fyb44wdhnd2ghhl.onion/ib/ - Onii-Chan

http://bx7zrcsebkma7ids.onion - Jisko

http://npdaaf3s3f2xrmlo.onion/ - Twitter clone

http://jv7aqstbyhd5hqki.onion - HackBB - Hacking & cracking forum

http://xdagknwjc7aaytzh.onion/20/http/1.4.7.9/forummain.htm - Read only access to the Freenet FMS forums via the Anonet Webproxy

http://sbforumaz7v3v6my.onion/ - SciBay Forums

http://kpmp444tubeirwan.onion/ - DeepWeb

http://r5c2ch4h5rogigqi.onion/ - StaTorsNet

http://hbjw7wjeoltskhol.onion - The BEST tor social network! File sharing, messaging and much more. Use a fake email to register.

http://t4is3dhdc2jd4yhw.onion/ - OnionForum 3.0 - New Onionforum for general talk, now with marketplace

http://zw3crggtadila2sg.onion/imageboard/ - TorChan - One of the oldest chans on Tor

Email and Messaging

http://bitmailendavkbec.onion - Swiss email

http://365u4txyqfy72nul.onion/ - Anonymous E-mail service. You can only communicate with other users currently using this service. So tell all your friends about it!

http://sms4tor3vcr2geip.onion/ - SMS4TOR - Self destructing messages

http://notestjxctkwbk6z.onion/ - NoteBin - Create encrypted self-destructing notes

http://torbox3uiot6wchz.onion/ - [TorBox] The Tor Mail Box

http://u6lyst27lmelm6oy.onion/index.php - Blue matrix chat NOT UP ALL THE TIME so chek often to see when it is

http://wi7qkxyrdpu5cmvr.onion/ - Autistici/Inventati

54

http://u4uoz3aphqbdc754.onion/ - Hell Online

Political

http://6sgjmi53igmg7fm7.onion/index.php?title=Main_Page - Bugged Planet

http://faerieuaahqvzgby.onion/ - Fairie Underground

http://2r2tz6wzqh7gaji7.onion/ - Kavkaz Center

http://tnysbtbxsf356hiy.onion/ - The New Yorker Strongbox

http://duskgytldkxiuqc6.onion/ - Example rendezvous points page

http://rrcc5uuudhh4oz3c.onion/ - The Intel Exchange Forum. Information and discussion on various topics, ranging from Illegal Activities and Alternative Energy, to Conspiracy Theories and Hacking. Same people from SnapBBS on a fully secure, moderated and categorized forum.

http://opnju4nyz7wbypme.onion/weblog/index.html - A7B blog :: a blog dedicated to the restoration of a limited constitutional republic in the USA

http://assmkedzgorodn7o.onion/ - Anonymous, safe, secure, crowdfunded assassinations.

http://duskgytldkxiuqc6.onion/comsense.html - Commo Sense by Thomas Paine

http://nwycvryrozllb42g.onion/ - Destination Unknown

http://zbnnr7qzaxlk5tms.onion/ - Wiki Leaks

Hacking

http://salted7fpnlaguiq.onion/ - SALT

http://yj5rbziqttulgidy.onion/ - Itanimulli

http://bbxdfsru7lmmbj32.onion/marketplace/ - Delta Initiative

Warez

http://2gxxzwnj52jutais.onion/ - The Nowhere Server (restored from backup after FH)

http://jntlesnev5o7zysa.onion/ - The Pirate Bay - Torrents

http://am4wuhz3zifexz5u.onion/ - Tor Library - library of books and other media files

http://uj3wazyk5u4hnvtk.onion/ - The Pirate Bay - Torrents (official .onion)

http://doxbindtelxceher.onion/ - DOXBIN
http://wuvdsbmbwyjzsgei.onion/ - Music Downloads
http://lolicore75rq3tm5.onion/ - Lolicore and Speedcore Music
http://xfmro77i3lixucja.onion/ - ebooks
http://vt27twhtksyvjrky.onion/ - lol 20th Century Western Music Recordings and Scores
http://2ygbaoezjdmacnro.onion/ - Pony at Noisebridge
http://xfmro77i3lixucja.onion/ - Imperial Library of Trantor
http://c3jemx2ube5v5zpg.onion/ - Jotunbane's Reading Club

Non-English

http://germanyhusicaysx.onion - Deutschland im Deep Web - German forum
http://ffi5v46ttwgx3fby.onion/ - Das ist Deutschland hier 2.0 - German Board
http://paisleli66axejos.onion/ - PAIS
http://runionv62ul3roit.onion/ - Russian Onion Union
http://s6cco2jylmxqcdeh.onion/ - ?ltimos bumps
http://5xki35vc4g5ts6gc.onion - GTF Greek Tor Forum . For greek speaking users
http://cipollatnumrrahd.onion/index.php - Cipolla 2.0 - Italian Community
http://runionv62ul3roit.onion - Russian community: market and anonymous talks about security, guns etc.
http://ptrackcp2noqu5fh.onion/ - PoliceTrack - Ne vous faites plus suivre par la police.
http://amberoadychffmyw.onion - Amberoad - russian anonymous market
http://r2d2akbw3jpt4zbf.onion - R2D2 - russian anonymous market
http://ramp2bombkadwvgz.onion - RAMP - biggest russian market (drugs only)
http://szmyt4v4vjbnxpg3.onion/ - Славянский
http://o2tu5zjxjlibrary.onion/ - Bibliotheca Alexandrina
http://xzzpowtjlobho6kd.onion/wordpress/ - DeepBlog
http://zqiirytam276uogb.onion/ - Thorlauta

7. The Toolkit

If you are using Tor – and require maximum security – do not install the browser directly onto any of your devices. Instead, install Tor onto a USB thumb drive or SD card and activate from there. In short, keep everything sensitive off your devices.

Portable Access

By using a USB, this will leave no trace on the actual computer used. These devices can be hidden or carried in a pocket to be used on an Internet-ready computer, including those in cybercafés and public libraries.

One of the most popular free solutions is Tails, which stands for The Amnesic Incognito Live System. It comes pre-configured with the Firefox browser, instant messaging, email client, office suite, image and sound editor, etc. However, installation is less than easy and there is a more practical solution given below.

Tails accesses the computer's RAM memory which is automatically erased when the computer shuts down, leaving neither trace of Tails nor your activities, but do read the *Warnings* page to understand the system's limitations.

You initially download an ISO image (archive file) that you later burn to a CD or install directly to a detachable drive. You will need to have set up a simple PGP Key first.

To burn an ISO image to disc for Windows, Linux or Mac, see the on-line brief *How to burn an ISO*. Full installation and running instructions for most operating systems can be found at the Tails website.

Alternatively, you may find it much easier to install the Tor/Firefox browser and any other useful programs directly to the detachable drive and then encrypt the drive with any one of a number of free programs.

There are numerous Windows-based tools including the open-source FreeOTFE which uses on-the-fly encryption, meaning data is automatically encrypted and decrypted without you having to do anything except enter a password.

Again, this is a little tricky to set up for 64-bit machines but the website has detailed instructions on how to do so. When installed, your USB drive will contain an encrypted volume where you can store sensitive data.

The program also includes the rather neat FreeOTFE Explorer, which allows you to circumvent administration restrictions on other peoples' machines, including those in cybercafés.

For the Mac users, the operating system has a built-in encryption tool. Simply plug in your USB drive and open up *Disk Utility* in the *Utilities* folder inside the *Applications* folder. Here you have a number of encryption options. You can also set the size of the volume, number of partitions and the format. Lock by password.

Sensitive USB drives should be fully encrypted. This is far more effective than encrypting individual files within the drive.

When a computer writes data to a USB drive, it uses what's called 'wear leveling', which means it sends data to random parts of the memory to prevent the same information blocks being used repeatedly and wearing out the drive.

As a result, when updated or new data is written to the USB, it can be sent all over the place, including to areas outside of the encrypted file. Equally, eraser programs may not be fully effective if you are just wiping individual files.

This means an adversary who can access the drive may also be able to access the unencrypted elements that have been randomly stored. When it comes to clearing data, the entire USB drive should be formatted and erased rather than erasing individual files.

Be sure to update software often to maintain security levels.

Free Portable Apps
This method is much easier: Install the Tor browser directly to a USB drive and then download the free PortableApps.com 'Platform' that bundles together a wide range of recommended open-source portable applications, from text editor to security software. Begin by downloading the Platform and then choose from the extensive list of apps. When running, a small dialogue box appears with access to the installed apps and to file storage.

Suggestions include:
- Notepad Portable Text Editor, with support for multiple languages.
- VLC Media Player Portable.
- IrfanView Portable, graphic viewer for Windows. View pictures, vector graphics, animated images, movies, icon files, etc.
- GIMP Portable, Windows image editor.
- Sumatra PDF Portable, lightweight PDF viewer.
- Eraser Portable, securely delete files and data.
- 7-Zip Portable, portable version of 7-Zip. Works with compressed 7z, ZIP, GZIP, BZIP2, TAR, and RAR files.

- AVG Anti-Virus Free.
- McAfee Stinger Portable, common virus and 'fake alert' remover.
- Spybot Search & Destroy Portable, Spyware detection and removal.
- CamStudio Portable screen recorder.
- Command Prompt Portable.
- Download with DownThemAll.

To keep sensitive data off your portable devices – documents, books, films, programs, etc – one option is to combine a secure Cloud service with a portable Operating System. There are an increasing number of Cloud stores now promising security and anonymity, options include Tresorit and Seafile. Install the PortableApps 'Platform' within a secure Cloud store, and only keep Tor on the drive. That way, there is nothing incriminating on your person and you can hand over encryption keys without fear of giving anything away. You just need to memorize the Cloud store location and login – accessing via the Tor browser. For those that like to run Linux, there is PenDriveLinux, a portable Linux operating system that runs off a USB.

8. Setting up Secure Comms

The Deep Web allows you to communicate much as you would on the Surface Web – via email, personal messaging and social networks, etc. On one level, your communications are scrambled by Tor and your IP address obscured, but other levels of security need to be added on top. You can mix and match options listed here to create a range of secure communications.

Email
As with everything else here, confine your sensitive email to a separate area. Do not use programs already installed on your computer such as Outlook. Instead, sign up with one of the many sites offering a free email service and access the account directly on-line or via a dedicated email program within a locked external drive.

The most popular of these is the Quicksilver Light for Windows and Linux, which is free. Using a high security protocol called *Mixmaster*, outgoing messages are multi-encrypted and sent through a series of email re-mailers which in turn strip away all traces of the email's origin and substitute their own. Quicksilver Email is said to be untraceable and unreadable to all but the intended recipient.

Additionally, Quicksilver only displays text, rather than HTML. This prevents you being caught by email marketeers and others using linked graphic files to track 'live' email addresses. HTML files and attachments are placed in a separate folder to be viewed offline.

Before downloading and installing Quicksilver, open a free mail account. A very good Surface Web option is unseen.is, an Icelandic-based free and subscription service offering 4096-bit encrypted email, chat, VoIP and file sharing. Another secure Swiss-based option is ProtonMail created in collaboration with scientists at Harvard, the Massachusetts Institute of Technology and the European research lab CERN. The compendium of *clearnet* email providers on the Hidden Wiki provides a detailed and current list of providers recommended by Tor users <!> http://kpvz7ki2v5agwt35.onion/wiki/index.php/Email.

Now download and install Quicksilver, following the set-up wizard, to access this account. There is also a version for Mac users.

Conversely, keep everything off your devices and drives by only ever accessing your email via a Web page interface. Additionally, email can be fully encrypted within the message, along with any attachments. See Encryption.

On-line email re-mailers where you can compose and send messages via a Web interface include awxcnx.de, cotse.net and Sendanonymousemail.

Bitmessage

Working on a similar system to BitCoin, Bitmessage is a decentralized, peer-to-peer messaging system that allows users to send encrypted messages to another person or to many subscribers. It uses strong authentication which means that the sender of a message cannot be spoofed, and it aims to hide 'non-content' data, like the sender and receiver of messages, from passive eavesdroppers. Bitmessage is simple to install and runs on most operating systems and on smartphones. Also ideal for installing direct to a USB thumb drive. This free, open-source program is available on the Bitmessage Wiki. For a detailed understanding on the system, read the white paper.

Secret Messaging
PrivNote — free Surface Web-based service that allows you to send top secret notes over the Internet. Requires no password or registration. Write a note and it will generate a link. Copy and paste the link into an email or PM and send. The recipient then clicks the link to see the note in their browser. The note then automatically self-destructs which means no one can read the note again, and the link dies. You can choose to be notified when your note is read.
SMS4Tor <!> http://sms4tor3vcr2geip.onion/ — just like PrivNote but on Tor.
SpamMimic — excellent free on-line tool that converts simple messages into *spamtext*, the kind of weirdly-written junk that arrives in everybody's email box and therefore looks totally innocuous. Simply compose a short message, hit the *Encode* button and out comes a load of nonsense which you cut and paste into an email. The recipient then pastes the *spamtext* into the *Decode* box and out comes the original message.

Even Deeper

Initially, investigators will be looking in the most obvious places, so communicate somewhere odd. An idea place is within the Usenet Newsgroups where messages and attachments can easily be hidden within innocuous-sounding groups. Other options include:

Freenet — free software which lets you anonymously share files, browse and publish Freenet websites. You can also do many of the usual things like chat on forums and post on boards. Freenet encrypts everything and routes it through other nodes to make it extremely difficult to determine who is requesting the information and what its content is. However, users are obliged to contribute to the network by giving bandwidth and a portion of their hard drive for storing files.

i2P — a little similar to Tor (in that it routes traffic through other peers and is encrypted end-to-end), i2P is an 'anonymizing network' using several layers of encryption, gives access to email services, peer-to-peer, IRC chat, and other things.

Hyperboria — free global, decentralized network offering secure communications and an "alternative to the Internet".

MMORPGs

A recent Edward Snowden revelation shows that the NSA and GCHQ have been infiltrating the realm of the Massively Multiplayer Online Role-Playing Games (MMORPG) in their attempts to track terrorists and money-launderers and, apparently, without any success.

However, it is unlikely that these agencies are monitoring every single conversation in Planet Arkadia or My Little Pony World.

With World of War Craft (WoW) drawing over 12 million participants and Second Life refusing to disclose any information about its residents, there are sizable crowds to hide amongst. At WoW, you can voice chat and PM as an Elf to an Orc; and few intelligence operatives are going to be watching you then.

Criminals and worse discovered these virtual worlds long ago and use them to launder money and make payments. Today, the virtual currencies of these two virtual worlds are so huge as to be listed on the real world currency markets. Who is to say you didn't mine a ton of virtual gold in the mythical land of Azeroth?

9. Encryption and Cryptography

Contrary to popular belief, the NSA and its British cyber partner GCHQ have not broken Internet encryption codes. What they have done is force some commercial encryption companies to install secret "exploits" such as "backdoors" into their programs and they have also hacked into various servers to steal encryption codes.

If an intelligence agency were capable of breaking full-on encryption then the mathematical community would soon know about it, and so would we.

Open-source encryption programs and services such as PGP are not affected and remain effective.

Data that can be read without special tools is called *plaintext* or *cleartext*. Hiding plaintext is called *encryption*. When plaintext is encrypted it turns to unreadable gibberish and this is called *ciphertext*. When you turn it back to its original plaintext this is called *decryption*.

Unencrypted email can easily be read or altered by someone with access to any of the computers along the route followed by the email.

PGP Public Key Cryptography — A **PGP Key** (Pretty Good Privacy) is a neat way to scramble data prior to emailing. It is also the most widely-used system.

Created by Philip Zimmermann, PGP is the standard program for secure e-mail and file encryption on the Internet. Originally designed as a human rights tool, PGP was published for free on the Internet in 1991. This put Zimmermann in trouble with the US authorities when PGP spread worldwide and apparently violated US export restrictions for cryptographic software. This is why you will find separate versions for the US market and elsewhere.

It works like this: you access any of several PGP programs and with it generate two keys – a public key and a private key. The public key you give out to anyone wanting to send you secure information. The sender uses your public key to encrypt the data and then sends it. When you receive the data, you unscramble it with your private key. The system is said to be totally secure and uncrackable. It also allows people to securely pass on data without any pre-existing security arrangements.

A typical PGP Public Key looks like this:

-
-----BEGIN PGP PUBLIC KEY BLOCK-----
Version: BCPG C# v1.6.1.0

mI0ET9YJ8wEEAI9MzWz7n8ipI/+owM/LeBON0cSGDpFs2XnVEX6goi/
/lpEfaLaZ
8Xedyx0oIgKfBinLkH6FCIOMdkXR+0aH1ZIxhT3JteAjweBfSPvEKCakf6P
6ZmFP
G2E5+3nzsv+8HnYfNCJtKNf11+OLFXbFjtLrxyG8SUZ6dLD3v2jA/0d1AB
EBAAG0
EnBncEBhbGFucGVhcmNlLmNvbcBdBABAgAGBQJP1gnzAAoJEBe21r
DUFUSDo9wD
/RvlfoTzM12lFU6aijwHCmZ8vMevydgPAwM4vJ8U8Jt+9rCWtq9V/oO0x
LvKRWuM
1PuTWiuCCtbukViQfVY3rVRyjCNnMYjNGRvb3D6ipbctxguE/KASLZSd
7yf5r08c
5OXh7LXbsu6bqnjv0fSUdytRXm70dosxDcs/4PglM/UA
=+IH0
-----END PGP PUBLIC KEY BLOCK-----

There are two free programs that you can run directly from your computer either as a standalone program or as an add-on to your dedicated emailer – GnuPG and PGPi – but these can be a little tricky to set up. Equally, those with 64-bit machines may find that the downloadable programs freeze or crash. A stable, commercial PGP version is available from Semantec that apparently works on Windows 7.

One of the easiest ways to incorporate PGP encryption into your emails and attachments is to use the free service offered by Unseen.is. You can generate both sets of keys and send and receive PGP encrypted emails with relative ease.

Also see the on-line guides, an Introduction to PGP and Secure Email Communication with PGP.

Alternatively, try GNUPG AT GNU Privacy Guard. See the Quick Start Guide for GNUPG installation instructions. Also, there is PGP4Win and a Mac version.

Disc Encryption/Erasure

The safest route for encryption is to encrypt the entire system drive, rather than individual files. Computer forensics can reveal a lot about your computer usage from the system partition including browsing history, bookmarks, emails and contacts details.

Investigators tend to focus heavily on contacts so it is important, not only to protect yourself, but those you are in contact with. If the investigator cannot access the hard drive their job is so much the harder.

Steganos Privacy Suite — not free but a good choice as it comes with numerous features: locks and encrypts drives or documents and photos, etc. Secures USB drives, CDs and DVDs, organizes and manages all passwords and access information. Shreds data so it cannot be reconstructed by recovery applications, plus Internet trace destructor.

Free Encryption Software:
> Kruptos 2
> Folder Lock
> Safe House
> Cypherix

Free Data Shredding Software:
> Eraser
> Evidence Nuker
> CBL Data Shredder
> Sure Delete
> DBAN

10. Steganography – hiding things inside things

Imagine receiving an email with a harmless photograph of your friend on vacation with her fiancé. But, known only to the two of you, there is a secret message hidden inside the image. This is steganography, the dark cousin of cryptography.

Steganography is the art of writing hidden messages in such a way that no one suspects the existence of the message. It comes from the Greek word *steganos* meaning *concealed writing* and its use goes back to the dawn of time. Think of invisible ink.

These days you can hide almost any kind of digital file by embedding it inside another digital file, such as a .jpg, .bmp or audio file.

It can be used for all manner of covert communication. WikiLeaks-type documents can be embedded inside a photo, short videos can be transmitted secretly inside a music file, and messages can be passed on by a digital 'drop box' held on a photo within a website.

Counter-technology isn't very good and there is little to give the game away unless the file is unexpectedly large. Just looking at the image or trying to open it with a steganalysis program will not show that the image contains any hidden data.

There are many data hiding packages and services available on the Surface Web for every operating system. OpenPuff is a good free program. A good source of information is the Neil Johnson website. To hide within an .MP3 bit stream, see MP3Stego.

Steganos Privacy Suite, as the name might suggest, includes the steganography program *Crypt & Hide* which is simple to use and works like this:

- Open the program and select *New Archive*.
- Add the file to be hidden (think about encrypting it first), click *Save*.
- Next click *Hide* to select a carrier file.
- Enter a password and save. The program will add the secret document to this image which you can then post. The recipient or viewer will need the same program and password to unlock it.

11. Transferring Secret Data

Downloading

Arguably, the best downloader option is DownThemAll which uses the FireFox/IceDragon proxy settings and so requires no configuration. Features an advanced accelerator that is said to increase download speed up to 400%. You can pause and resume downloads. It also allows you to download all the links or images on a webpage and customize the search criteria. Ability to download a file from different servers at the same time for additional security.

Privoxy is a Web proxy service that fetches items (Web pages, images, movies, etc) and passes them on to you when complete.

The Tor Browser will warn you before opening or downloading items handled by external applications.

If you want to maintain your cloak, do not open documents downloaded through Tor while online, especially .doc and .PDF files as these can contain all manner of nasties that reveal your true IP address. To access downloaded files, first disconnect your computer from the Internet. Never use Tor and BitTorrent together, see BitTorrent and Tor.

Uploading

Uploading sensitive material is a little more risky than downloading it so extra care should be taken. Always connect to Tor before uploading. Individual files, such as text or images, should be placed inside a RAR or 7z file and encrypted.

Large files, such as AVI, DivX, etc, should be split into several components before uploading. Use HJSplit, a free program that both splits and re-joins large files.

Never upload all the parts to the same server/host as they can be spotted and opened. Instead, upload to as many different servers/hosts as possible.

Give each part a different name. The recipient should know to rename them in the correct order so they can then be un-split. Do not give the files any name that identifies the content.

Hosting, Storing & Sharing

Host your own Deep Website without revealing your IP address to users by configuring the Tor control panel. This way you can use your own computer, or preferably another separate one, to host the website. For additional security, the website might only be available at certain predefined times. Configuration is a little complex and requires the knowledge to set up a Web server locally. See the on-line guides Configuring Hidden Services and Tor Hidden Service Protocol.

However, keep it ultra-simple and construct a Web page and then save it as a single image file or as an HTML document. This can then be uploaded to any of the file sharing sites below, and the image address distributed.

You can also do much the same thing on the Surface Web with pastehtml.com. With this on-line application you can construct simple websites using text, images and links by selecting the *Formatted Text* option. Conversely, if you can work in HTML code, you can drop that in directly. You can register an anonymous domain name elsewhere and set it to link directly to the pastehtml address and retain the original domain in the address bar.

Real Hosting — <!> http://hosting6iar5zo7c.onion/ hosting service paid with BitCoin.

TorShops — <!>http://shopsat2dotfotbs.onion/ create your own .onion store. BitCoin payment.

Liberty's Hackers — <!>http://libertygb2nyeyay.onion/ BitCoin hosting service.

Cyrusery — <!>http://cyruservvvklto2l.onion/ BitCoin hosting service.

OnionWeb File Hosting — <!>http://3fnhfsfc2bpzdste.onion/

Prometheus Hidden Services & Hosting — <!>http://prometh5th5t5rfd.onion/

OneSwarm — P2P file sharer where you can select who to share with.

RetroShare — securely chat and share files using a 'web-of-trust' to authenticate peers and OpenSSL to encrypt communication, plus PMs, forums and other channels.

12. Smartphones

If you want to be monitored 24/7 and followed wherever you go, buy a smartphone.

Mobile espionage, long the preserve of law enforcement and specialized investigators, has now evolved into a fully-fledged cybercrime industry. In 2011, Kaspersky Labs detected nearly 5,300 new malicious programs for all mobile platforms. By 2012, the total number of unique malicious files exceeded six million – the vast majority aimed at Android. Today, the number is almost beyond count.

Threats come in three main forms – SMS Trojans, adware, and exploits to gain control of the device. Smartphones can also be infected when connected to compromised computers and vice versa. Avoid free charging points.

Additionally, law enforcement may oblige the service provider to remotely reprogram a phone's air card allowing for precision tracking. This technique, generically known as 'stingray' or IMSI catcher, allows agents to spoof a legitimate cell tower and trick the smartphone into connecting directly to the stingray. Stingrays are now being deployed in unmanned aerial vehicles.

The majority of malware comes hidden inside seemingly harmless apps which run in the background and collect data all day long. Malicious programs have been detected in apps on Google Play and the App Store for iOS.

They will track your locations, browsing and downloads, and collaborate with other running apps to build up a detailed profile. Some will intercept incoming calls or activate the microphone. Many apps harvest contacts, some collect passwords, while others send secret messages to premium-rate numbers, running up your charges. Worse still, there are apps that run even when the phone is switched off.

Most apps are free or very cheap because developers make their money by allowing in ad networks and other malevolent parties. Be alert when an app asks permission to use your current location – many don't bother to ask – and never give out email addresses or other personal information.

A growth area in mobile malware is SMS spam where unsolicited messages plant Trojans that hijack the device or just trick users into revealing personal information. As with email and social networks, never open attachments or follow links unless you know them to be safe.

Ironically, viruses are commonly hidden inside smartphone security software. Only install programs from the industry leaders like Avast, Trend Micro and Kaspersky, etc. For a list of recommended smartphone security apps, visit the CTIA website.

Whilst the iPhone is an excellent tool, it does have its limitations when it comes to security. Data is stored internally and cannot be removed, nor can the battery. There are spy apps they work even when a device is seemingly switched off.

Counter-Intrusion

For Android users, a good free option is AVG Mobilation which protects against viruses, malware and spyware. It also identifies unsecure device settings and advises on how to fix them; ensures contacts, bookmarks and text messages are secure; checks media files for malicious software and security threats; guards against phishing; and offers anti-theft protection. Lost or stolen smartphones can be found via Google Maps, plus you can turn your phone's GPS on remotely and have the device send its location to you. You can also lock your phone remotely.

Lookout protects iOS or Android devices from unsecure Wi-Fi networks, malicious apps, fraudulent links, etc. You can also use it to back up your contacts by scheduling automatic backups and then accessing the information online, or using it to restore your device in case of a crash or data loss. If you lose your phone, Lookout can locate it on Google Maps – even if the GPS is off and the phone is on silent.

For iOS, the Anti-Virus & Malware Scanner does much the same as AVG Mobilation but additionally lets you scan files on remote locations such as Dropbox and web servers. Trend Micro also offers good mobile security for Android.

- Put a security code on your smartphone in addition to the SIM code and engage the auto-locking feature.
- Disable network connections and switch off bridging connections. Do not broadcast the Bluetooth device name and disable automated peer-to-peer Wi-Fi connections.
- Turn off Geotagging and GPS location via *Settings*.
- Whenever possible, access 2G, 3G or 4G networks in preference to free Wi-Fi services.
- Do not store sensitive files on the phone's internal storage. Encrypt data onto the SD card or hide in a secret compartment.

- Enable remote-find or remote-wipe features.
- Do not 'Jailbreak' any device – the act of removing limitations through software or hardware exploits.
- Avoid connecting personal devices to the office network or computer. Avoid free charging points.
- Watch for unauthorized charges, rapidly-depleting battery and unusual text messages.
- If you link your smartphone to your car's on-board computer, be sure to regularly delete sensitive information, contacts and travel history.
- Employ a mobile data backup service, such as Trend Micro.
- Update models regularly to keep the operating system in line with security enhancements.
- Remove battery or leave your phone behind when meeting contacts, etc. If meeting in a group, do not all remove the battery at the same time as this appears ultra-suspicious to anyone observing any members of the group. The battery cannot be removed from an iPhone but it can be run down until completely flat and then resurrected with a portable battery. Remove the sim card, too.
- When attending demonstrations, etc, replace the SD card in the phone with a spare that does not contain personal data and contacts in case of arrest. Also, switch to Airplane Mode to avoid being tracked.

007 Apps

The smartphone in your pocket can easily be turned into a high-tech spy tool and counter-surveillance device to rival anything that Ian Fleming's Q might have dreamt up. You can secretly record, access banned content and communicate securely, particularly so if used with an unlocked phone and an unregistered pay-as-you-go sim card.

You can take your smartphone onto Tor and keep everything off-radar using apps for Android and iOS with access to both Deep and Surface Webs, plus PM and email without being monitored or blocked. However, you will not be able to access certain sites this way if they insist on JavaScript. Be sure to adjust the security settings as shown above.

In certain situations, such as a demonstrations and riots, Tor-enabled mobiles can still connect to social networks and websites which may be blocked by the government. However, most social networks make heavy use of JavaScript which will give your identity away but Twitter does have a mobile facility as does Facebook Mobile which do not use JavaScript and can, therefore, be accessed anonymously. Facebook also has a Dark Net presence at <!> https://facebookcorewwwi.onion.

Scramble Calls — Silent Phone for Android and iOS provides HD quality securely-encrypted phone/video communication over any network – 2G, 3G, 4G, WiFi. RedPhone offers end-to-end encryption for Android. Signal from Open Whisper Systems is a free version of Redphone providing end-to-end encrypted text and VoIP calls for iOS and Android. Highly rated but needs tweaking to make it as safe as possible. See the configuration guide at DeepDotWeb. Unseen has also introduced a secure audio and video conferencing facility that promises high end security. Jitsi is a free, open-source VoIP service for audio/video and chat that supports protocols such as SIP, XMPP/Jabber, AIM/ICQ, Windows Live, Yahoo!

Secret Messenger — there are secret messaging systems for all devices. Secret SMS for iOS will encrypt messages between users and hide them. Perzo is a new encrypted messaging system for all devices. There is also Signal Private Messenger for Android. SureSpot is an encrypted messaging system for Android and iOS that also allows you to send photos and audio clips. Delete a message and it is also deleted on the recipient's phone. Telegram is a free, open-source messaging app for Android and iOS with end-to-end encryption and a self-destruct feature.

Secret Image — Top Secret Video Recorder for Android and iOS allows you to seemingly switch off the smartphone while continuing to film. A quick examination of the phone will not show any activity. You can also make and receive calls while the camera is secretly running. ReconBot for Android is a stealth video, photo and audio recorder that displays a black screen while it records. Includes remote view so you can watch the recording live via a web link. Also includes location data.

Remove Image Data — if you want to upload images that cannot be traced back, you need to remove or alter the EXIF data which most modern cameras implant in the image to give GPS location and other details. Options for Android include the ExifEraser and ViewExif for iOS. 'Geotagging' can be turned off in most Android and Apple mobile devices by going into the *Settings*.

Secret Audio — there is Secret Voice Recorder for Android and Spy Recorder for iOS which can also automatically record when you enter certain locations that you set with Google Maps. The Top Secret Audio Recorder for iOS is a covert recorder that looks like a regular picture-viewing app. You can swipe through the photos but as soon as you tap on an image the recording begins. The recordings can also be password protected.

Record Calls — Top Secret Call Recorder for Android and various versions for iOS.

Ear Spy — convert your smartphone into a covert listening device by amplifying the sound around you. With Bluetooth headphones you can also leave your device in one room and listen in while in another. Free and paid-for versions for Android and iOS.

Confirm Contacts — if you receive a call and want to know who actually called, add them to a *Contacts* file and check them out with Contact Spy for Android and iOS which lets you quickly search people or companies by running them through this search engine app for web entries, images, news, blogs and US-only physical addresses.

Secret Compartment — secret folders for Android and iOS. Protect sensitive data by storing it in a hidden and encrypted file.

Location Trackers — helpful for dangerous assignments, GPS tracking allows for real-time monitoring of a phone's location via Google Maps. Some, like GPS Tracking Pro for Android and iOS, have a check-in feature so you can let the office know you are okay. Also highlights nearby safety points like hospitals.

Panic Button — Amnesty International has introduced an app disguised as a calculator that automatically issues a call for help when the user repeatedly presses the 'On' button, sending SMS distress messages to three previously-set destinations. Currently only available for Android.

See in the Dark — enhanced night vision photography and live feeds with the Night Vision Camera for Android and iOS. Works best on cameras with a good-quality lens.

Police Scanner — there are several police and emergency service scanner apps. Police Scanner for Android taps into scanners from around the world. For iOS, Radio Police Scanner does much the same.

Track Planes — Plane Finder – Live Flight Status Tracker for iOS and Android displays thousands of flights globally using real-time ADS-B signals used by aircraft to transmit their positional data. Enter flight number or tap on the map showing the planes above your head.

Chart Vessels — monitor the position of all manner of vessels from passenger and cargo ships to yachts and gin-palaces. Ship Finder – Live Vessel Tracking for iOS and Android picks up AIS position data from around the world and provides details and photographs of the vessels.

Mobile VPN — to cover your back, there is Hotspot Shield which encrypts all smartphone and tablet traffic through a Virtual Private Network (VPN) to mask your identity and prevent tracking (not recommended for use with Tor because it puts strain on the network). It also allows you to view banned content and access Twitter and Facebook mobile if their services are ever blocked locally.

Wipe Clean — Complete Wipe is an Android app that securely wipes a phone of sensitive data at the click of a button.

Remove Evidence — there are shredders for Android and iOS.

Self-Destruct — perhaps the ultimate weapon in Q's arsenal is the self-destruct feature. The free Wickr app allows you to encrypt any data – text, pictures or videos – and then have them self-destruct once unscrambled and viewed, leaving no trace for the forensic investigator. Available for Android and iOS.

Additionally, there is now a regular Firefox browser for both Android and iOS. Use this in preference to the browser that came bundled with your device. Also, install various security apps from within the Mozilla domain.

13. Usenet Newsgroups

Newsgroups may not carry much news but are a rich source for all manner of media files that other people have posted and which you can download without drawing anyone's attention. They are also ideal for surreptitious communications.

Usenet Newsgroups are a bit like an email system where anybody can post on any subject and anybody else can read those messages or download attachments. You need special Newsreader software and a low-cost subscription to the network. It can be installed on any operating system and in most modern devices.

Usenet – which remarkably has been around since 1980 – has been largely ignored by Internet users probably because it does not have the same glitzy appeal of the World Wide Web but rather resembles an endless list of discussion topics, which is precisely what you do see.

But Usenet is Deep Web and it is secure if you take the right precautions. It can defeat Deep Packet Inspection (DPI) technology because it prevents the ISP from seeing inside your data by using secure 256-bit SSL encryption. Although your ISP can tell if you are accessing Usenet, once you pass beyond the curtain, everything you do there is hidden from inspection.

There are Newsgroups devoted to every conceivable subject from *alt.fan.jackie-chan* and *alt.aviation.jobs* to *alt.binaries.sounds.mp3.world-music*.

The most popular Usenet Newsreader software is Free Agent, available in both free and paid-for versions. A network subscription costs US$4.99 per month upwards and gives access to an enormous store of digital material going back years, offering a better option than torrents for downloading without drawing attention.

Just type newsgroups into Google or iXQuick and compare thousands of offers. To see what is available, check out the search engine at binsearch.info.

A popular provider is Giganews http://www.giganews.com/ with bundled Mimo newsreader and add-ons, including the useful and speedy Vypr Virtual Private Network (VPN) which further masks you on Usenet and allows you to browse the Surface Web with a degree on anonymity by pretending to be in any one of six countries.

Downloading from Usenet is secure, in that nobody can see what you are doing. However, if you wish to add extra levels of security, consider the following:

Do not use credit cards or PayPal when signing up with a Usenet provider. Many will accept the BitCoin, leaving you free to write what you like in the contact details.

Sign up using Tor so they cannot see where you are coming from (but do not combine Tor and Usenet access as this places strain on the Tor network).

Add a VPN that accepts BitCoins to mask your activities from your ISP. Consider Mullvad VPN.

Avoid signing up with any companies based in the United States.

Install the Newsreader and VPN onto a USB thumb drive and access them from there.

Using the Russian Doll principle, communications can easily be hidden by placing them inside any group you like, preferably the dullest possible. By placing your message in the group *alt.emircpih.pets.porcupines* and giving it a header that no one will want to open such as *Spam-Buster Pro,* you will have placed a needle inside the vastest of all possible haystacks that nobody without prior knowledge will ever be able to find.

14. Producing videos and stills

When you take a photo on a modern digital camera, smartphone or tablet, certain information is embedded within the image which can be used to identify you.

If you are uploading and transmitting sensitive images you will need to modify the EXIF data otherwise an adversary can easily discover all sorts of things, including the make and model of the camera used, the date the image was taken, whether it was modified and by which software. It can also show if the photo was taken by a professional or an amateur, and even where it was taken if the camera logs GPS coordinates.

Innocent family photos uploaded to the Web often contain GPS data on the image's EXIF file, allowing others to pin-point a location.

If this is a concern, you will need to modify the image's EXIF file, which isn't too difficult. EXIF is short for Exchangeable Image File and almost all new digital cameras and smartphones store data this way.

You can check how much data is stored in a digital photo by uploading one of your own to an on-line application such as exifdata.com, which allows you to take a deep look inside.

There are numerous free tools to help you modify EXIF files:

ExifTool
JHead
IrfanView
jStrip

'Geotagging' can be turned off in most Android and Apple mobile devices by going into the *Settings*. GPS information is not generally stored in video cameras, although this is likely to change. If giving away the location is an issue, be sure to avoid landmarks, and audio tracks that pick up the local radio or TV.

Video code can be modified and the size of the file reduced by using HandBreak, an open source, multiplatform video transcoder.

Conversely, all TV news channels feature what they describe as 'unverified' images and video footage which viewers have sent in. The fact that these news items cannot be verified denudes the validity of the material.

To help identify the video, try to add locations that can be recognized. Traditionally, kidnap victims used to hold up a copy of a newspaper to prove they were alive on a given date. Similar principles can be applied to video tracks by adding TV or radio broadcasts and copies of newspapers, etc. When filming an event, pan the camera around at the end of the sequence to capture landmarks. This will help verify authenticity.

15. Basic Computer Security

Avoiding Viruses, Trojans and Spyware

Infections are easily contracted by email so it is important to put a range of security measures in place. Quicksilver is an excellent freeware email program for the security-conscious. See Email/Re-Mailers.

Always Disable HTML in your emails via the *Settings* tab. Look for and untick *Display attachments inline* or tick *View message body as...plain text*.

Among the most dangerous forms of malware that can infect your computer are Key Stroke Logging programs and, in extreme cases, tiny hardware versions that can be hidden inside your computer. These work by logging every keystroke and mouse movement you make.

Physical devices tend to be inconspicuous and may sometimes resemble a USB plug or lay hidden deep inside the machine. An option is to apply a drop of paint to the screws at the back of the keyboard and computer unit so you can see if it has been tampered with.

If you fear a key logging program may be placed inside your device, KeyScrambler offer several solutions, including a free option, to scramble your keystrokes and defeat surveillance.

Other malware can tap into your computer's microphone or webcam and send back a live transmission.

Use Anti-Virus software to scan incoming emails. Do not open attachments while on-line as this can open you to scrutiny.

Use a combination of standalone security software with one firewall, one or two Anti-Virus programs, and one or two Anti-Spyware program. Also consider using dedicated anti-Trojan software. Avoid running in 'real-time' to avoid software conflicts and, instead, regularly scan your computer.

It is also prudent to secure your home and office wireless networks. The simplest solution is to change the administrator password for the wireless router. Hackers can look-up the manufacturer's default password and easily break in, intercepting all the data you send and receive.

You should also refer to the router's handbook and switch off SSID (Service Set Identifier) broadcasting and change the default SSID name to something not easily identifiable. It is essential to keep firmware updated and to use WPA2 encryption rather than WPA or WEP.

USB Internet modems should be used with extreme care following a recently discovered vulnerability allowing an attacker to execute malicious code remotely by sending an SMS message to the victim, allowing access to the target's computer.

When choosing a password, select a memorable phrase rather than an actual word that can be found in a dictionary. For example, I Like Lots Of Vinegar On My Fish And Chips can be written as ILLOVOMFAC. You could add to this numbers and non-alphanumeric characters and a mix of upper and lower case. If you have a UK-English keyboard, use the £ symbol for its rarity value. Therefore, £ILLOVOMfac! could stand as your basic passphrase and then add on an identifier such as £ILLOVOMfac!Am@z for Amazon.

You might also choose a line from a favorite poem or a passage from a book. This, in turn, can also be used as a means of passing on a password. Once the recipient understands the principle, you just mention any book that can be found on Amazon. They look inside and read the relevant line to receive the password.

Recommended Free Programs:
As a rule, free, open-source software is preferable to the paid-for variety because developers and others can have a good look inside for backdoors and other things that should not be there. All proprietary encryption software should be treated with the upmost caution.

Comodo Personal Firewall — free and paid-for versions of combined anti-virus and firewall programs. The firewall application uses cloud-based data to analyze new programs and data to prevent attacks. It protects against viruses, Trojans, worms, hacker attacks and other threats.
Lavasoft's Ad-Aware — free and paid-for versions. Provides core protection against Internet threats. Featuring real-time anti-malware protection, advanced Genocode detection technology, rootkit protection and scheduler.
Spybot Search and Destroy — free, fully functioning privacy and anti-malware software. The program checks your system against a comprehensive database of adware and other system invaders. Immunize feature blocks a range of uninvited Web-borne nasties before they reach your computer. Also includes Secure Shredder, Hosts File which blocks adware servers from your computer, and System Startup which lets you review which apps load when you start your computer.
AVG Anti Rootkit — removes Rootkits, a malicious program somewhere between a virus and Trojan horse which opens your computer to external attack.

Crap Cleaner — free system-optimization tool. It removes unused and temporary files, allowing the computer to run faster and more efficiently with more hard-disk space. The application cleans traces left by Windows, Internet Explorer, and third-party applications.

Avast Free Antivirus — full-featured software with the same antivirus and anti-spyware scanning engine used in Avast's premium products.

AVG Anti-Virus Free Edition — probably best of the bunch when it comes to free anti-virus software.

In all these programs, be sure to check the *Settings* and turn off *automatic updating*. Manually update at regular intervals.

What's Running Now?
Always keep an eye on which programs are running on your computer, especially for anything new that starts up when you switch on. In Windows, open the *Task Manager* by right-clicking on the taskbar and selecting the *Processes* tab. To compare what is running on your machine against what it should typically run, see whatsrunning.net.

With Windows, you can also check to see which programs are set to start when you boot up by going to *Start/Run* and entering *msconfig* in the box. To compare your list with the most likely start up applications, see the Start Up Applications List.

Freeware options for viewing your start up items and running processes, include Process Explorer and CurrProcess.

Zero Emission Pads

Surveillance teams can remotely scan the electromagnetic signals from a computer monitor and reassemble the screen image. They can do this through walls and over long distances. These signals are called *compromising emanations* and in surveillance jargon the art of capturing them is known by the code word Tempest.

As a surveillance tool, this is less popular in the West because of the sheer amount of electrical equipment transmitting in the 100KHz - 2MHz range and because people have moved away from CRT monitors to LCD.

You can prevent people looking in by using a Zero Emission Pad – a software program which defuses the compromising rays. Available in a Freeware version.

For more modern screens, adversaries can bombard an area or room with a Continuous Microwave Generator that effectively connects the target computer to an outside monitor. Place a towel or similar to obscure the screen.

Cleaning Up

The Heidi Eraser is freeware that allows you to completely remove sensitive data from a Windows hard drive by overwriting it several times with carefully selected patterns. The *Erase Secure Move* feature erases all traces after you move files from one place to another. Eraser can also be set to erase the Windows *pagefile* on *shutdown/restart* and it has the option of being added to your context menu, so when you right-click a file, you can select *Erase*.

Erasing History

Almost every piece of software wants to store information about you and what you like to do. Internet browsers keep a record of your browsing history and downloads. PDF readers store a history of the files you've read. MS Office records recently opened documents and words in the documents. Media players store details of recently played files.

To erase your tracks in one go consider dedicated cleaning software like CCleaner. When choosing software, select one that gives you the option to specify the number of times data is overwritten. A minimum of three 'passes' is recommended.

Windows OS
Windows is no longer supporting its XP operating system which means there will never be another security update. It is now more vulnerable than ever. For those addicted to Windows, upgrade to Windows 8.1.

Windows, because it is designed for the mass market, is an inherently insecure operating system that runs a lot of unnecessary services that can put your computer at risk. As a result, it is best to disable any unused services. Doing so will also help increase the speed of your computer.

> First, open the *Computer Management* window
> Right-click *My Computer*
> Click *Manage*
> Expand *Services and Applications*
> Select *Services/Standard* tab

If any service status shows *Started*, and you are not using it, click *Actions* and then the *Stop* button. If you are unsure, read the item *Description*. If still in doubt, leave as is. To change from *Automatic* to *Manual*, etc, click *Action*, *Properties*, *General*. Then click on *Apply* and *OK* when you have finished.

Application Management — set to Manual.

Automatic Updates — for downloading and installing Windows updates. Disable if you think you don't need this service.

ClipBook — Disable

COM+ Event System — Disable if you are not programming in Visual Studio .NET. If you are programming in VS .NET set to Manual.

COM+ System Application — Disable if you are not programming in Visual Studio .NET. If you are programming in VS .NET set to Manual.

Computer Browser — Disable. This lists all computers on a network and gives information to other computers on the same network. This service is unnecessary and, even while Disabled, you can still browse the network.

Distributed Link Tracking Client — Disable if you are not on a network. This is only applicable when you use the NTFS file system. If you don't, you can switch off this service.

Error Reporting Service — Disable. This reports system errors to Microsoft.

Fax Service — Disable if you do not use the internal fax machine.

Help and Support — set to Manual.

Human Interface Device Access — Disable.

IPSEC Services — Disable if you are not using remote connection to a company network.

Messenger — Disable. This service has nothing to do with Live Messenger.

Net Meeting Remote Desktop Sharing — Disable. This service opens your computer to inspection and control by others computers as a remote desktop.

Network DDE — Disable.

Performance Logs and Alerts — Disable.

Protected Storage — Disable. This service stores passwords which can be easily retrieved.

Remote Access Auto Connection Manager — Disable.

Remote Desktop Help Session Manager — Disable.

Remote Registry — Disable. This service allows external users to make changes to your registry keys.

Removable Storage — set to Manual.

Routing and Remote Access — Disable.

Security Center — Disable. This service monitors the functioning of your system security (Windows updates, firewall and virus scan).

Server — Disable if you are not on a network.

System Event Notification — Disable.

System Restore Service — Disable. This service allows Windows to restore your system to an earlier date and opens your computer to inspection from different points in the past.

Themes — Disable.

Windows Image Acquisition (WIA) — Disable. This service transfers images from your camera/web cam or scanner.

Wireless Zero Configuration — Disable if you are not using a wireless connection.

Windows Security Center

Window's own built-in Security Center and Firewall are woefully ineffective and should be Disabled via the Control Panel and replaced with a third party firewall instead.

Pagefile/Swapfile

By default, Windows creates a file on your hard drive (pagefile.sys) which it uses as additional computer memory. Most modern computers, those with over 1GB of RAM, don't need this so it should be Disabled. Go *Control Panel, System, Advanced* tab, then select the *Settings* button under the *Performance* heading, *Advanced* tab, *Virtual Memory, Change,* select *No Paging File,* click *Set,* then *OK.*

Hibernation

Windows Hibernation Mode needs to be Disabled as it saves current data to your hard drive in plaintext which can then be retrieved. Go *Control Panel*, *Power Options*, *Hibernate* tab, then uncheck *Enable Hibernation*.

Alternative Software
Microsoft's own software leaks like a sieve and is best replaced with the open source variety. Avoid using Office, Outlook, Internet Explorer, and Windows Media Player as they collaborate with each another.

Use Open Office Suite instead of MS Office (Word, Excel, etc). Always Disable *auto-save* in the program options.
Use VLC Media Player instead of Windows Media Player.
Use Foxit PDF Reader instead of Adobe Acrobat Reader. Be sure to tick *Enable Safe Reading Mode*. And untick *Restore Last View Setting when Reopening*.

Linux users should read the on-line Linux Security HowTos.
Mac users should visit the SecureMac website.

16. Deep Currency

Transferring money without leaving a trace is not always easy. However, the Deep Web's own currency the BitCoin may provide the solution. Not just for paying off hit men or buying industrial quantities of horse tranquillizer, the BitCoin can be used for all sorts of on-line transactions from ordering flowers to buying karaoke equipment.

This is electronic money, a crypto-currency that does away with the need for banks by combining a limited quantity digital currency with state of the art cryptographic security and a peer-to-peer network. All transactions are irreversible. It is also free, unlike Visa or PayPal.

How does it work? It's a little complex but in essence BitCoin is open-source software invented by Satoshi Nakamoto that logs all transactions on the network and records them on the so-called Blockchain. The first BitCoins were issued on January 3, 1998.

The number of BitCoins is limited by the design of the network. There will never be more than 21 million BitCoins which means they are likely to increase in value unlike conventional currencies such as the US Dollar and Euro, which are daily diluted and devalued by quantitative easing.

The value of a BitCoin is determined by the automated online markets which match buyers and their bid prices with sellers and their asking prices.

BitCoin transactions are anonymous and identified only by their BitCoin address, which need not link to any existing conventional account. However, when making payments to an exchange or bank account, the BitCoin address may link back to you – opening all your digital transactions to scrutiny. In which case, open a number of BitCoin addresses and move the money around them first. You can have as many BitCoin addresses as you wish.

Because there is no single issuing authority, there is no single point of failure which, in today's climate, can only be a bonus. If your bank goes under, you may lose your money but it's unlikely that the Internet will collapse any time soon and take down the BitCoin network.

Payments are sent with one click like email and are just as swift. Accounts cannot be frozen and nobody need know what you are buying. BitCoin recognizes no national boundaries nor has limitations on where money can be sent.

You can use BitCoins online for millions of items and even make donations to charities. You can also make purchases at physical shops and restaurants that accept them. See the BitCoin trade wiki for a list of online and real world businesses.

BitCoins can be purchased in the same way that you buy any currency. You can ask your bank to buy them for you or pay via Visa or Western Union, etc. They can also be bought and sold with a mobile app. For a full list of exchanges, see the wiki on Buying BitCoins.

They are also infinitely divisible. You can send someone 0.00000001 of a BitCoin for a very small item or any amount that you hold.

Some people see them as a good investment. Back in December 2010, one BitCoin was worth about US$0.22. Since then the currency has risen to soaring heights and slipped down again but it is still worth considerably more than it was at launch. See the BitCoin Exchange Rate website.

The BitCoinMe.com website has detailed FAQs on using BitCoins. For a detailed time-line history of BitCoin see http://historyofbitcoin.org/.

Useful Links

Avast - https://www.avast.com
Hotspot Shield - https://www.hotspotshield.com
Signal - https://whispersystems.org/
Smartphone Spy Apps -
http://www.hongkiat.com/blog/iphone-spy-apps/
Ear Spy - http://www.overpass.co.uk/app/ear-spy/
Ship Finder - http://shipfinder.co/about/
Tresorit - https://tresorit.com/
Seafile Secure Cloud Storage -
https://www.seafile.com/en/home/
FinSpy - https://wikileaks.org/spyfiles/files/0/289_GAMMA-201110-FinSpy.pdf
Fake Tweets - http://www.lemmetweetthatforyou.com/
Expand Short Links - http://checkshorturl.com/
No More Ransom - https://www.nomoreransom.org/
Angry IP Scanner - http://angryip.org/
Shodan - https://www.shodan.io/
Philips HUE lighting system - http://www2.meethue.com
Mozilla Firefox - https://www.mozilla.org/en-US/firefox/new/
Firefox Add-Ons - https://addons.mozilla.org/en-US/firefox/
Open Office Suite - https://www.openoffice.org/
VLC media player - http://www.videolan.org/vlc/index.html
Foxit PDF Reader -
https://www.foxitsoftware.com/products/pdf-reader/
Recommended VPNs – https://www.deepdotweb.com/vpn-comparison-chart/
Tor Onion Browser - https://www.torproject.org/
Evidence Nuker - http://www.evidencenuker.com/
AnonyMouse Email Remailer -
http://anonymouse.org/anonemail.html
Unseen Email - https://unseen.is/
PrivNote - https://privnote.com/#
PGP Pretty Good Privacy - http://www.pgpi.org/

Platform Operating System - http://portableapps.com/download
Recommended Search Engines - https://duckduckgo.com/ and see http://www.howtogeek.com/113513/5-alternative-search-engines-that-respect-your-privacy/
Newsbin - http://www.newsbin.com/
Usenet - http://www.usenet.com/
OpenStego - http://www.openstego.com/
Deepdotweb - https://www.deepdotweb.com/
Hidden Wiki - https://thehiddenwiki.org/

Also recommended:
http://www.wonderhowto.com/

Part 2 - Deep Search
Introduction

When it comes down to it, there is no great mystery to the Deep Web. It's a big place, for sure, but there are notable landmarks to help you find your way around. This 'hidden' Internet may be made up of squillions of petabytes of data stored around the planet but very little is truly hidden. You just need to know where to look.

For the everyday things, Google and the conventional search engines do a good job. But detailed information is not always easy to find, especially when the engines throw up thousands of pages of results. Most people rarely venture beyond the first page or two and after 14 minutes of fruitless looking even the most determined usually give up.

Understanding how to interrogate any search engine will certainly help. But knowing where to look is often more important.

The regular search engines only index a tiny fraction of the data stored on the Internet. They do this by extracting the 'visible' data on websites. This is then searchable with keywords.

The information held on the Deep Web is largely contained inside databases and archives and this content is not indexed by the conventional engines because they are rarely programmed to enter these data stores. As such, this so-called "Deep Web" information can only be found by interrogating the database or archive directly through their own search facilities. The archives themselves can usually be found by asking a conventional Surface search engine to find them for you.

For example, suppose a Boeing 767 crashes and you want to look for similar incidents. You would begin your search in the conventional way with Google, asking it to find a database dealing with air accidents and, hopefully, it will point you to the Aviation Accident Database. The data held within this site is, therefore, Deep Web because it will not have been indexed by the Surface search engines so they won't know what is inside. But, once there, you can enter the make and model of the aircraft, along with a daterange, and pull up every accident report for every incident globally, along with all the probable causes. Trying to do this by interrogating a Surface search engine alone would take more time than most people are ever likely to devote.

The same thing works for historical documents and quotations. For example, you may come across the line "I am the most unhappy man. I have unwittingly ruined my country" and want to pin it down. Google will certainly provide the apparent quote by Woodrow Wilson – *"I am the most unhappy man. I have unwittingly ruined my country. A great industrial nation is now controlled by its system of credit. We are no longer a government by free opinion, no longer a government by conviction and the vote of the majority, but a government by the opinion and duress of a small group of dominant men".*

But what you see is not necessarily the actual quotation and you will also see endless examples of people regurgitating the line without pinning it down to a time and a place or to a specific document. You will also see a lot of debate as to its validity because most people do not know how to search effectively. But, by knowing that Woodrow Wilson said this, Google can find the right archive, taking you to woodrowwilson.org where you can quickly track part of the line down to a 1912 campaign speech and find the remainder in the full-text version of Wilson's book *The New Freedom* published in 1913, the year he signed the Federal Reserve into existence. You could spend all day on Google and achieve nothing, as opposed to 20 minutes of reading in the right archive.

So it is not that difficult. You just need to know where to look and, of course, how to phrase the right question.

It would be difficult for this book to list every possible archive and database and all the other portals within the Deep Web, but below you will find some of the most useful. For the rest, ask a conventional search engine.

2.1 How to Search

Searching on the Deep Web is just like searching on the Surface Web. You need to know where to look, how to phrase your question and how to refine the search; so it helps to understand the main types of search service out there and how they work.

As obvious as it might seem, web searching is a matter of selecting the right words and devising a strategy to find what you are looking for. Unfortunately, not all search engines use the same rules but it helps to understand the basic way most engines work. Google, for example, uses Boolean logic, as do many of the popular engines. The examples below will work for most of them.

Phrase Search — by putting double quotes (" ") around a set of words, a Boolean engine knows to consider the exact words in that exact order. An example might be "fish and chips" which will show all documents containing that same phrase (12 million results), rather than all documents containing the word *fish* and all documents with the word *chips* (40 million results). Engines tend to ignore the word *and* when lower-case because it is too common to log. You can also use double quotes to track down documents that you know contains a specific phrase, such as "Under the Federal Reserve Act panics are scientifically created". By wrapping this sentence in quotes, Google and other Boolean engines will find around 20,000 documents containing a quote from 1929 by adventurer and Congressman Charles Lindbergh, whose baby son was famously kidnapped. This is effectively half the results if you had typed the sentence without the quotes. This also works for names. The query "George Bush" will throw up over 70 million results, but take the quotes away and you have more than 225 million to choose from.

Excluding Words — a minus sign (-) immediately before a word tells the engine that you do not want pages containing this particular word. If you want to know more about Charles Lindbergh but want to remove all references to the kidnapping of his baby son in 1932, you would type "Charles Lindbergh" -kidnapping. This will reduce the results by about 200,000. Some engines prefer the word NOT in place of the minus sign, such as "Airedale Terrier" NOT breeders (note Google prefers the – sign, while AltaVista is happy with either).

Wildcard — the asterisk symbol (*) tells the engine to treat the asterisk as a missing word and to come up with the best matches. Typing Google * will call up a list of all of Google's services, from Google Translate through to Google Sky. The asterisk is also handy when looking for a word that has variants, like *smoking* but you would also like to see references to *smokers*, *smoke* and *smoked*. Try *smok**.

Using OR — by using the word OR in capital letters, engines can serve up a range of variables. To find a library or archive devoted to Lindbergh you would type "Charles Lindbergh" library OR archive and thereby widen your scope. Some engines prefer not to use OR but use the | symbol instead.

Using AND — another seemingly obvious one but something often neglected in web searches. By adding the word AND (or with some engines the + symbol) to a search phrase, specific elements are added to the search. Typing "Charles Lindbergh" AND economy will bring up results linking him with the economy. However, if we wanted to exclude results about fuel economy, we would add a minus sign: "Charles Lindbergh" AND economy -fuel.

Search within a website — Boolean engines can be asked to search within a specific website for their results. Typing Afghanistan site:www.time.com will produce a breakdown of all references to Afghanistan in Time Magazine.

Domain Search — domains are broken down by country, such as *.af* for Afghanistan and *co.uk* for the United Kingdom, and by type of organization such as *.org* for non-profit making organization or *.edu* for education in the United States. Typing "hamid karzai" site:af will bring up everything listed on sites with an Afghan domain referencing the President. Typing Afghanistan site:gov will return results only from a US *.gov* domain.

Search by Document Type — often detailed information, especially studies and reports, can be found by seeking out particular document types. A request for Afghanistan filetype:PDF will offer only PDF files. Typing Afghanistan filetype:ppt will give results for PowerPoint Presentations, and *xls* for spreadsheets. Be alert that certain files types – MS Word, Excel and PDF especially – may contain viruses and should be opened with caution. Where possible, use the *View as HTML* option.

Search Titles — many engines give you the option to search for keywords in the title of documents. intitle:Afghanistan AND landmines will take you to all documents but these will also include news reports. Reduce this by typing intitle:afghanistan AND landmines filetype:ppt and you will be offered only PPP documents that contain these words in the title. Also be aware that different ways of spelling will influence the results, so you might want to type intitle:Afghanistan AND landmines OR "land mines". Using *allintitle* restricts results to documents containing all the keywords. For example allintitle:afghanistan drugs warlords.

Synonym Search — by inserting a tilde (~) in front of a word, most engines will search for the word and its synonyms. A search including the words *computer ~security* will also produce results covering encryption, malware, firewall, etc.

Search in URLs — website addresses (URLs) often contain clues to their subject matter, so you can seek out websites devoted to particular issues. For example, inurl:Airedale will offer websites purely devoted to the King of Terriers.

Related Site Search — using *related:* will bring up a short list of sites either similar to or in some way related or linked to a particular website, for example related:www.airedale.com.

Reverse Link Searching — websites and databases that you find particularly useful are often linked to by other equally interesting sites that you might also want to explore. To find out which sites link to the Internet Movie Database, for example, type link:www.imdb.com.

Cache Search — to search for sites and pages that no longer exist, typing cache:www.airedale.com will show the last stored version of that page.

Lucky Search — adding certain types of words to a search can produce interesting results, especially when you are looking for documents that may have been inadvertently posted online. These include "not for distribution", "company proprietary", "confidential", "secret", etc. Typing filetype:xls site:za confidential will produce several hundred pages of confidential business information from South Africa.

Search by Date — not easy as most engines do not have a facility to date search. Often, if dates do show up, they refer to the last time a particular page was indexed rather than created or modified. The ability to search by date is helpful as it allows you to weed out older documents and select the latest versions or search for news stories around a particular time. You can type in *daterange:* and then the date but most engines operate on Julian Time, a scientific system of time measurement, so you will need a Julian Time converter. The date 7 July 2000, for example, appears as 2451733.06531. To make matters worse, decimal points confuse most engines, so you have to drop the point and the last five digits. If we want to pin down the Afghan president to a particular time-frame, say the first two days of April 2012, we would input daterange:2456019-2456020 Hamid Karzai (or Hamid Karzai daterange:2456019-2456020) and now we have just 13,000 results to choose from and a better chance of refining the search further. (Additionally, it may help on some engines to drop the quotes around phrases when using *daterange*.) However, while this works for contemporary characters, it is less successful with historical ones. If we want to find out what Charles Lindbergh was up to between 20 May 1927 and 20 June that year, we would type "Charles Lindbergh" daterange:2425021-2425052. While this does narrow down the search, it is far from satisfactory as it includes many dates outside that range.

The Exalead search engine has a date search facility that allows you to search *before* and *after* dates, i.e. Mohammed Karzai before:2004/05/21 and Mohammed Karzai after:2004/05/21.

You can search specifically for PDF files including ebooks via dedicated search engines:
PDF Search Engine
PDF Searcher

Data Sheet
PDF Geni
PDF Database

PowerPoint presentations can be found via these engines:
Slideworld
SlideFinder
JpowerPoint
PPT Finder
PPTSearch365

2.2 Search Engines

Search engines work by storing key information from the webpages that they retrieve using an automated web browser known as a Crawler. This information is extracted from the site's title page, content, headings and meta tags. Results are generally presented in list form and can cover webpages, images and some file types. A few engines also mine data inside databases but coverage is a long way from comprehensive.

Some search engines like Google store all or part of the source page (known as a cache). Others, like AltaVista, store every word of every page they find. When a user enters a query into a search engine, the engine examines its index and provides a listing of best-matching webpages, usually with a short summary containing the document's title and sometimes some of the text. The engine looks for words or phrases exactly as entered.

Most search engines rank their results to provide the "best" results first. How a search engine decides which are the best pages tends to vary.

Most search engines are in it for the money and some charge advertisers to have their listings ranked higher. Those which don't charge make money by placing search-related ads alongside the regular search results and get paid whenever someone clicks on an ad.

Google Alternatives — Google, along with most search engines, stores detailed information about your interests. Each year, the FBI compels these companies to hand over the personal details of hundreds of users without presenting a court order. There are, however, alternative engines that do not store information on you in the first place:

IxQuick
Startpage
DuckDuckGo
Secret Search Labs

Secure Addons for Firefox:
StartPage
Scroogle

Deep Web Search — no single engine can search the entire Deep Web and no single directory can cover it all, but these go some way:
InfoMine — built by librarians at the University of California, California State University, the University of Detroit-Mercy, and Wake Forest University.
Librarians' Internet Index — search engine listing sites deemed trustworthy by librarians.
SurfWax — practical tools for dynamic search and navigation.
BUBL — catalogue of Internet resources.
Pinakes Subject Launch Pad — academic research portal.
Search.com — dozens of topic-based databases from CNet.
OAIster Database — millions of digital resources from thousands of contributors.

Metasearch Engines
A good way to perform a detailed search is to employ a metasearch engine to search multiple search engines simultaneously. These include:
DogPile
Mamma
Kartoo

Database Search — there are specialized search engines for finding databases. Arguably the best of the bunch is CompletePlanet which scours over 70,000 searchable databases and specialty search engines. Other notables include:

Search.com — seeks out databases and allows you to search multiples engines with a single query.

TheInfo.com — search specific engines and databases.

Beaucoup — one of the first specialized search engine guides, listing over 2,500 selected engines, directories and indices.

FinderSeeker — breaks searches down by country and even cities.

Fossick — covers over 3,000 specialized search engines and databases.

Databases and Gateways

Repositories of Primary Sources — direct links to over 5,000 archives, databases and websites globally.

WWW Virtual Library — first catalogue of the web, started by Tim Berners-Lee in 1991. Run by a loose confederation of volunteers.

Librarians' Internet Index — compiled by librarians offering a searchable, human-reviewed gateway to quality sites in the Surface and Deep Webs.

Digital Librarian — a librarian's choice for the best of the web's databases and research resources.

GPO — US Government Printing Office, access to multiple databases including records, hearings, reports, manuals, court opinions, etc.

Library of Congress Catalogs — gateway to a vast collection of academic institutions, universities, libraries, and miscellaneous databases.

CIA Electronic Reading Room — search for declassified CIA documents.

Project Vote Smart — database of US government officials and candidates.

USPTO — patient full-text and image database.
US Census Bureau International Database — demographics, world population data, etc.
WebLens — portal to academic and scholarly research papers and thousands of useful Internet research tools.
DOAJ — Directory of Open Access Journals, free full-text scientific and scholarly journals, covering numerous subjects and languages.
Geniusfind — directory of thousands of search engines, databases and archives organized into categories and subcategories.
Ask Eric — education resources information center.

Open Directories — assembled by human beings who use editorial judgment to make their selections and not by Crawlers running algorithms. A web directory is not a search engine and does not display lists of webpages based on keywords but divides the web into categories.
The categorization is usually based on the whole website rather than one page or a set of keywords. Most directories are general in scope and list websites across a wide range of subjects, regions and languages. But some niche directories focus on countries, languages, industries, products, etc.
Popular directories include the Yahoo! Directory and the very comprehensive Open Directory Project.

User-Edited Directories — are compiled, as the name suggests, by users who are generally experts in their field and who wish to share favorite sites and improve search results. These include IllumiRate and JoeAnt.

2.3 Search Sources

People Search

There are a range of specialty search tools for tracking down individuals. Most concentrate on the US but these will often pull up people from elsewhere on the planet, depending where they are listed.

Pipl — the best place to begin a search. Pipl casts a very wide net, searching within social networks, websites, blogs, magazines and newspapers, phone and public records, background checks, criminal records and even within classified advertisements. Works well internationally.

Yoname — good, across-the-board people search internationally.

Spokeo — primarily a US-based search facility with email and username search and reverse address and telephone look-up.

Abika — again, primarily US but very detailed search including criminal records by state, county and Federal, also global civil and criminal search, tax records, mortgages, evictions, background checks, personality profiles, traffic violations, vehicle history; plus image, audio and video search.

Zaba Search — also US but claims to offer three-times more residential listings than the White Pages. Also offers reverse phone lookup.

Public Records — a gateway to public records across the US.

Find County Records — directory of US county public records.

Jail Base — free and paid-for service offering jail inmate searches across the US.

123people.com — free international people search including social network usernames.

192.com — excellent paid-for people and business search in the United Kingdom.

Find My Past — search family records from Britain, Ireland, Australasia and the US. Subscription service.

UK National Archives — covers births, death and marriages, military records, employment,   Census, etc.

Numberway — links to international White and Yellow page phone books.

FoneFinder — free, international reverse telephone number lookup.

Social Network Search

Topsy — excellent service which allows you to search for Twitter users across Twitter and other media, viewing their entire tweet timelines and references to them, etc. Also allows for date and language search.

Monitter — real-time Twitter search tool that allows you to monitor Twitter for mentions of any words or phrases, people, places or usernames, and from specific locations.

Facebook Directory — search people listed publicly on Facebook.

Social Mention — search trends across social networks and receive email alerts – covers people and celebrities, products, brands and companies, news events, etc.

Paid-for Search Services

Cision — comprehensive people watching service with real-time monitoring and analysis reports covering blogs, micro-blogs, social networks, forums, video and image-sharing sites, news sources, print and broadcast media. Track the impact of a story, identify key developments, trace individuals across the web.

Sysomos — business intelligence for social media, provides instant access to all social media conversations from blogs, social networks and micro-blogging services to forums, video sites and media sources.

Business Search

FT Search — search the Financial Times' archives, company profiles and business news with over 10 million full-text articles from 2,000 different European, Asian and American business sources. US$10 per month.

TechRepublic — the web's largest library of free technical IT white papers, webcasts and case studies. Covering data management, IT management, networking, communications, enterprise applications, storage, security, etc.

GuideStar — information on 640,000 non-profit organizations including recent tax returns.

Foundation Center — providing information on over 70,000 foundations, including grants. Look up organizations, identify funding sources, check statistics.

Kompass — search products, services and companies.

Economic Search

EconoMagic — links to over 400,000 data files with charts and excel files for each. Broad coverage including economic forecasts, indicators, reports, etc.

Free Lunch — free economic, demographic and financial data.

eFinancialBot — global search engine for financial resources.

Science and Engineering Search

Scirus — said to be the most comprehensive scientific research tool on the web. With over 545 million scientific items indexed, search for journal content and scientists' homepages, courseware, pre-print server material, patents and institutional repository and website information.

TechXtra — find articles, websites, books, industry news, job announcements, e-journals, e-prints, technical reports, research, thesis and dissertations.

E-Print Network — integrated network of electronic, scientific and technical information created by scientists and research engineers. All full-text searchable. Gateway to over 35,000 websites and databases worldwide, containing over 5.5 million e-prints in basic and applied sciences, primarily in physics but also chemistry, biology and life sciences, materials science, nuclear sciences and engineering, energy research, computer and information technologies.

Science Research — comprehensive public SCIENCE and technology research portal, searching over 300 collections globally.

Science.gov — search over 55 databases and over 2,100 selected websites from 13 Federal agencies, offering 200 million pages of US government science information including research and development results.

WorldWideScience — search portal to international science databases in multiple languages.

CiteSeer — database of technical and scientific literature sponsored by the School of Information Sciences and Technology at Penn State University.

NTIS — National Technical Information Service offers a keyword-searchable database of unclassified government-sponsored technical and scientific reports. Reports are downloadable and generally cost under $20.

Medical Search

MedBioWorld — resource portal for professional medical and biotechnology information.

UCLA Health — information resources for physicians and staff.

PubMed — comprises more than 22 million citations for biomedical literature from MedLine, life science journals and online books.

DrugBank — vast database of medicinal drugs.

Art Search

Musee du Louvre — find works at the Louvre, the Department of Prints and Drawings, and works in French museums.

Guggenheim — searchable database of selected artworks from the Guggenheim's permanent collection. The site contains more than 1,100 artworks by over 450 artists. Also includes works from the Peggy Guggenheim Collection Venice, and the Guggenheim Museum Bilbao.

National Portrait Gallery — more than 100,000 portrait records from the Catalog of American Portraits, a survey of American portraits in public and private collections across the US and abroad. National Portrait Gallery collections are included in this database.

Smithsonian National Portrait Gallery — find portraits for more than 80,000 people in this database.

Your Paintings — the entire UK national collection of oil paintings and the stories behind them. The digital archive is made up of paintings from thousands of museums and other public institutions around Britain.

Image and Media Search

Internet Archive — superb digital library offering free access to books, movies, music and sound recordings, as well as 271 billion archived webpages. Includes the WayBack Machine for a snapshot of websites from different points in their past.

PicSearch — image search service with more than 3,000,000,000 pictures.

Yale University Library — access over 500,000 digital images.

Harvard University Library — vast historical image collection.

NYPL Digital Gallery — open access to over 800,000 images digitized from the New York Public Library's vast collections, including illuminated manuscripts, historical maps, vintage posters, rare prints and photographs.

TinEye — reverse image search. Enter an image and see where it exists on the web.

Sonic — Library of Congress Recorded Sound Collection contains 2.5 million audio recordings on a variety of formats representing the history of sound recording from late 19th century cylinders and discs to digital files, include radio broadcasts and spoken word, as well as vocal and instrumental music.

BeeMP3 — search engine for locating mp3 audio files with over 800,000 in the database.

blinkx — vast video search engine.

MetaTube — browse 100 of the most popular video sharing sites simultaneously.

Miscellaneous Search

Public Library of US Diplomacy — searchable database of over 1.7 million US diplomatic files from 1973 to 1976, including diplomatic cables, intelligence reports and Congressional correspondence, courtesy of WikiLeaks.

The Spyfiles — WikiLeaks database of hundreds of documents from over 160 intelligence contractors in the mass surveillance industry.

Digital Public Library of America — over two million archived books, images, records, and sounds.

AgriSurf — agriculture and farming search site.

USDA — researchable database of all plant life in the USA.

FindLaw — search cases and legal news.

Galaxy of Knowledge — search the Smithsonian Libraries for digital content, books, images, etc.

EFF — the Electronic Frontier Foundation, protecting civil liberties in the networked world. On this site are white papers and a searchable archive.

CDT — The Center for Democracy and Technology is a non-profit public policy organization providing data on legislation affecting the Internet, works to promote democratic values and constitutional liberties in the digital age.

Project Gutenberg — searchable catalog of over 20,000 full-text books for free.

Internet Public Library — search resources by subject, newspapers and magazines, collections, etc.

US Census Bureau International Database — demographics, world population information, etc.

Genome — information on genomes including sequences, maps, chromosomes, assemblies, and annotations.

Europa Press Releases — find press releases from the European Union.

MagPortal — find individual articles from many freely accessible magazines, browse by categories or search facility.

Penn World Tables — international purchasing power parity and national income for 189 countries.

Aviation Accident Database — information from 1962 onwards for civil aviation accidents and incidents internationally. Generally, a preliminary report is available online within a few days of an accident.

The Sherlock Holmes Handbook for the Digital Age
Sherlock Holmes is the greatest detective of all time. He is
driven to right the wrongs of the world. It is only natural that
he should turn his attention to the Internet.

"The Internet has become a sinister and dangerous place – a
grotesque parody of all that it originally promised," explains
Holmes. "Open your eyes, Watson. We are living in a
postmodern surveillance dystopia from which escape for all
but the most skilled individuals is impossible."

Luckily, Holmes has all the right answers. This is a cyber-
security and digital counter-surveillance handbook like no
other.

Our two heroes embark on a perilous journey to the Dark Side
learning along the way to avoid the traps laid by their
adversaries – the State, the Corporate Giants and the
Criminals and Insane.

From self-destructing messages to anonymous browsing, we
visit alternative Internets and discover how to employ the
Dark Arts for the power of good.

This is a Call to Arms. The time has come to reclaim the
Internet from the commercial interests, the scammers and the
surveillance state. And – as Sherlock Holmes clearly
demonstrates – it is really simplicity itself.

This book may only take a few hours to read but it will change
your life.

Buy on Amazon

———

Other Books by Deep Web Guides
*

Deep Web for Journalists – Comms, Counter-Surveillance, Search
By Alan Pearce

Can you guarantee to protect your sources?
Do you know how to scramble your phone calls?
Can you send and receive secure emails?
Do you know how to mask your identity online and browse anonymously?
Can you store data securely and keep your emails and contacts out of the hands of law enforcement?

Being a journalist in 2017 is more dangerous than it ever was. In addition to the usual threats, beatings, murders and war casualties we are now being actively targeted online by intelligence agencies and law enforcement.

These days it is not just journalists working in repressive regimes that need worry. Increasingly, outwardly-democratic governments are tightening control over the Internet and those who use it.

Start researching terrorism or other sensitive subjects and a tracking device will quickly be planted in your computer to follow you around and report back. It is all too easy for an algorithm to misconstrue your browsing activities and for alarm bells to be set off.

Not every journalist needs be concerned about this. But it is important to know how to operate securely should you ever need to. If you can't offer confidentiality, you are compromised.

Rather like spies in a James Bond movie, journalists have an array of digital tools to call upon, both to mask their identity and to provide real confidence that their correspondence, notes and contacts are secure.

There are smartphone apps that let you see in the dark or measure the height of a building. You can film and record without being discovered; scramble your calls, and send emails and texts that cannot be intercepted. You can access banned websites and even take over and control public and private security cameras.

Journalism has been transformed by the Internet and the Internet has opened journalists to levels of surveillance that would have horrified George Orwell. All journalists should be aware of the dangers they face in the digital world – the emerging battleground.

Deep Web for Journalists "offers an uncompromising diagnosis of the perils of online communications and should shatter the confidence many of us place in the unguarded ways of working online," says Jim Boumelha, President of International Federation of Journalists in his Foreword to the book.

"This engaging book by Alan Pearce charts a path to online knowledge which should be compelling reading for all journalists."

Deep Web for Journalists – Comms, Counter-Surveillance, Search by Alan Pearce will be available from most online book stores and direct from Deep Web Guides.

ENDS

20663287R00075

Printed in Great Britain
by Amazon